Forgotten Books

A Simplified Grammar of the Ottoman-Turkish Language

By

James W. Redhouse

Published by Forgotten Books 2012

Originally Published 1884

PIBN 1000102910

TRUBNER'S COLLECTION OF SIMPLIFIED GRAMMARS OF THE PRINCIPAL ASIATIC AND EUROPEAN LANGUAGES.

EDITED BY REINHOLD ROST, LL.D., Ph.D.

I.
HINDUSTANI, PERSIAN, AND ARABIC.
By the late
E. H. PALMER, M.A.
Price 5s.

II.
HUNGARIAN.
By I. SINGER.
Price 4s. 6d.

III.
BASQUE.
By W. VAN EYS.
Price 3s. 6d.

IV.
MALAGASY.
By G. W. PARKER.
Price 5s.

V.
MODERN GREEK.
By E. M. GELDART, M.A.
Price 2s. 6d.

VI.
ROUMANIAN.
By R. TORCEANU.
Price 5s.

VII.
TIBETAN.
By H. A. JASCHKE.
Price 5s.

VIII.
DANISH.
By E. C. OTTE.
Price 3s. 6d.

IX.
OTTOMAN TURKISH.
By J. W. REDHOUSE.
Price 10s. 6d.

Grammars of the following are in preparation :—
Albanese, Anglo-Saxon, Assyrian, Bohemian, Bulgarian, Burmese, Chinese, Cymric and Gaelic, Dutch, Egyptian, Finnish, Hebrew, Kurdish, Malay, Pali, Polish, Russian, Sanskrit, Serbian, Siamese, Singhalese, Swedish, &c., &c., &c.

LONDON: TRÜBNER & CO., LUDGATE HILL.

A

SIMPLIFIED GRAMMAR

OF THE

OTTOMAN-TURKISH LANGUAGE.

BY

J. W. REDHOUSE, M.R.A.S.,

HON. MEMBER OF THE ROYAL SOCIETY OF LITERATURE

LONDON:

TRÜBNER & CO., LUDGATE HILL.

1884.

LONDON:

GILBERT AND RIVINGTON, LIMITED,

ST. JOHN'S SQUARE, CLERKENWELL ROAD.

TABLE OF CONTENTS.

CHAPTER III.

The Ottoman Syntax.

ERRATA.

PAGE					
10,	l. 22,	*for*	مَدّ	*read*	مُدّ
16,	l. 18,	*after*	å	,,	&c.
24,	l. 15,	*for*	أُاب	,,	اَاب
28,	l. 4,	,,	جَزم	,,	جزم
29,	l. 2,	,,	پرنْس	,,	پِرنْس
,,	l. 9,	,,	شِدّت	,,	شِدّت
,,	l. 9,	,,	مَدّ - عطّار	,,	مَدّ - عطّار
,,	l. 10,	,,	وَدّ	,,	وِدّ
,,	l. 16,	,,	عطّار ، بَقّال	,,	عطّار ، بَقّال
30,	l. 1,	,,	پَرّ	,,	پَرّ
31,	l. 19,	,,	رأس	,,	رأْس
35,	l. 2,	,,	ابتدا	,,	اِبْتِدا
47,	last line,	,,	أ	,,	ا
54,	l. 18,	,,	رُويَان	,,	رُويَان
91,	l. 10,	,, VIII....Verb	,, IX....Conjug: p. 100		
124,	last line,	,,	اوليَحَق	,,	اُوليَحَق
127,	first line,	,,	تَپمش	,,	تَپمش
154,	l. 3,	*add:*	(See p. 73, l. 4.)		
168,	l. 7,	*for*	جنَابلَری	*read*	جنَابلَری
In pp. 10—16		,,	ٔ	,,	٥

PREFACE.

THE Ottoman Language, عثمانليجه osmanlïja, is the most highly polished branch of the great Turkish tongue, which is spoken, with dialectic variations, across the whole breadth, nearly, of the middle region of the continent of Asia, impinging into Europe, even, in the Ottoman provinces, and also, in Southern Russia, up to the frontiers of the old kingdom of Poland.

The Ottoman language is, in its grammar and vocabulary, fundamentally Turkish. It has, however, adopted, and continues more and more to adopt, as required, a vast number of Arabic, Persian, and foreign words (Greek, Armenian, Slavonic, Hungarian, Italian, French, English, &c.), together with the use of a few of the grammatical rules of the Arabic and Persian, which are given as Turkish rules in the following pages, their origin being in each case specified.

The great Turkish language, تركجه turkje, Ottoman and non-Ottoman, has been classed by European writers as one of the "agglutinative" languages; not inflecting its words, but

"glueing on," as it were, particles, "which were once independent words," to the root-words, and thus forming all
the grammatical and derivative desinences in use.

To my mind, this term "*agglutinative*" and its definition,
are inapplicable to the Turkish language in general, and to
the Ottoman Turkish in particular. These are, essentially
and most truly, inflexional tongues; none of their inflexions
ever having been "independent words," but modifying particles only.

The distinctive character of all the Turkish languages, or
dialects, is that the root of a whole family, however numerous,
of inflexions and derivations, is always recognizable at sight,
seldom suffering any modification whatever, and always standing at the head of the inflexions or derivations, however
complex in character these may be. When a modification
of a root-word does take place, it is always of the simplest
kind, always the softening of a hard or sharp consonant into
the corresponding more liquid letter, and always of the final
consonant only of the root. Thus, a ت or ط sometimes
becomes a د, a ق becomes a ك, a sharp Arabic ك becomes a
soft Persian گ, or the Ottoman modification of this latter,
which is then pronounced like our most useful consonant *y*,
or, in case of a dominant *o* or *u* vowel in the root, is pronounced like our consonant *w*.

The Ottoman Turkish has more vowel-sounds (eleven in number) than any other tongue known to me. As each of these may have a short and a long modification, they make twenty-two possible vowels in all. Every one of these is distinguished by a special mark in the transliterations of the present treatise, though it is impossible to attempt any such differentiation in the Arabic characters to which the Ottoman language is wedded.

The rules of euphony regulate the pronunciation of every word in the Ottoman language; perfectly, in all of Turkish origin; and as far as is practicable, in what is radically foreign.

Although a compound word is a thing totally unknown to the Turkish dialects, and of very rare occurrence in Arabic, the Ottoman language abounds with such, adopted from the Aryan, compounding Persian.

Persian grammarians and writers first learnt how to mould into a harmonious whole the incongruous Aryan Persian and Semitic Arabic elements. Ottoman ingenuity has gone a step further, and blended in one noble speech the three conflicting elements of the Aryan, Semitic and Turanian classes of vocables.

Fault is found by some with this intermixture of idioms;

but an Englishman, of all the world, will know how to appre-
ciate a clever mosaic of diction ; and a real student of the
language will learn to admire many a true beauty, resulting
from a masterly handling of the materials at his command,
by any first-rate Ottoman literary celebrity, whether prose-
writer or poet.

NOTE.—The manuscript of the present sketch Grammar was completed
before Christmas, 1882, and copies of my table of identic alphabets have been
in the hands of a few friends for the last four or five years. I have just
had the pleasure and privilege of reading the admirable and exhaustive
treatise on "The Alphabet," by the Rev. Isaac Taylor, and am rejoiced to
find that he has come to the same conclusion as to the identity of the
three ; probably at an earlier date than the time, perhaps twenty years ago,
when the idea began to force itself on my mind. I still feel inclined
however, to hold by the inference that the Phenicians gave the alphabet
to Italy, quite independently of the Greek action which later on doubtlessly
influenced the Italian culture.

LONDON,
September, 1883.   J. W. R.

OTTOMAN TURKISH GRAMMAR.

CHAPTER I.

THE LETTERS AND ORTHOGRAPHY.

SECTION I. *The Number, Order, Forms, and Names of the Letters.*

THERE are thirty-one distinct letters used in the Ottoman language. Some of these have more than one value; and four of them are sometimes consonants, sometimes vowels. There is also a combination of two letters into one character, ﻻ or ﻻ, la, which Arabian piety has agreed to count as a letter, and which Persian and Turkish conformity has had no option but to adopt. Thirty-two letters have, therefore, to be named and enumerated, as follows:—

ا elif, ب be, پ pe, ت te, ث se, ج jim, چ chim, ح ha, خ khi, د dal, ذ zel, ر ri, ز ze, ژ zhe, س sin, ش shin, ص sâd, ض dad, ط ti, ظ zi, ع 'ayn, غ gayn, ف fe, ق qaf, ك kaf, ل lam, م mim, ن nun, و wâv, ه he, ﻻ lam-elif, ى ye.

The foregoing is the ordinary arrangement of the letters of the Ottoman alphabet, as learnt and repeated by children;

excepting that they are not at first taught to mention, or to know, either of the three Persian letters, پ pe, ـچ chím, and ژ zhe, which are not contained in the Arabic alphabet, their sounds and values being unknown to, and unpronounceable by, an Arab. It is called the elíf-be, القِ بِ, i.e., *the alphabet;* and it might be conveniently styled the *alphabet by forms;* letters of the same form being brought together in it, more or less.

There is another very different order necessary to be learnt of the twenty-nine Arabic letters. It is called ebjed, اَبْجَد, and is arranged in eight conventional words, as follows : اِبْجَد ebjed, هَوَّز hevwaz, حُطِّي hutti, كَلَمَن keleman, سَعْفَص sa'fas, قَرَشَت qáráshát, ثَخَذ sákház, ضَظَغَلا dázágílá.

The letters of the Arabic alphabet, as arranged in this ebjed series, have each a numerical value. The first nine in order represent the nine units, 1 to 9; the second nine stand for the tens, also in order, 10 to 90; the third nine count as the hundreds, serially, 100 to 900; the twenty-eighth in the series, غ, stands for 1000; and the last, لا, though always enumerated, has no value of its own, but counts as the sum of the values of its two components, ل 30, ا 1; *i. e.*, as 31.

This system appears to have been in use in very early times indeed. The order of the letters in it is that of the Hebrew alphabet, as far as this goes; that is, as far as the end of the sixth word qarashat, قَرَشَت, with which the Hebrew alphabet terminates. The letters of the two last words (omitting now all consideration of the factitious ي) are Semitic inventions of a comparatively modern date, and are modifications, by means of dots, of letters, undotted or dotted, represented in the Hebrew alphabet. Thus, ت is modified from ت, ـ is from ـ, ذ from د, ض from ص, ظ from ط, and ج from ح. This may be called *the numeral alphabet*.

A circumstance that invests this ebjed arrangement with a European antiquarian interest of the very highest order, is the fact that it proves, beyond the remotest shadow of a doubt, the unity of origin of the Semitic (usually taken to be Phenician, but I imagine it to be much more ancient than Moses, or even Abraham), the Greek, and the Latin alphabets. Not only can the now divergent forms of each separate letter in the series be traced through successive modifications back to one ancient Phenician character, but the order of the whole series from ا to ت is absolutely identical in the Arabic (Hebrew, Phenician), Greek, and Latin alphabets, as the following synopsis shows. An additional proof is furnished by the identity of the numeral values of the letters in the Arabic and Greek alphabets,—a method totally unknown to the Latins, who must have had a method of their own, probably Etruscan, before they received their alphabet direct from the Phenicians, quite independently of the Greeks, and quite as early.

Arabic.	Greek.	Num.	Latin.	Arabic.	Greek.	Num.	Latin.
ا	A	1	A	ع	O	70	O
ب	B	2	B	ف	Π	80	P
ج	Γ	3	C	ص	–	90	–
د	Δ	4	D				
ه	E	5	E				
و	Ϛ	6	F	ق¹ 100	Ϙ	90	Q
ز	Z	7	G	ر 200	P	100	R
ح	H	8	H	ش 300	Σ	200	S
ط	Θ	9	–	ت 400	T	300	T
ى	I	10	I	ث 500	Υ	400	U
ك	K	20	K	خ 600	Φ	500	V
ل	Λ	30	L	ذ 700	X	600	X
م	M	40	M	ض 800	Ψ	700	–
ن	N	50	N	ظ 900	Ω	800	Z
س	Ξ	60	–	غ 1000	ϡ	900	–

The apparent discrepancies and vacancies occurring on comparison of the three alphabets and the series of numerals, are in reality additional proofs of their absolute identity.

The two first letters call for no remark, though it is known to scholars that the Greek B has been degraded in Rumaic into a *V*, and the so-called modern Greek man is unable to pronounce a *b*, writing it, when necessary, μπ. This combination in Greek words he reads and pronounces as though it were written υβ.

---

¹ The Hebrew system is identical with the Arabic as far as its alphabet goes. Thus: ק 100, ר 200, ש 300, ת 400; beyond this the words are written in full. This incident is a condemnation of the Greek system for the higher numbers.

The ⌣, Γ, G, must originally have been a *hard g*. In modern Egyptian, as in Hebrew, and in Greek, it is so pronounced, though the rest of Arabia has softened it into the sound of our English *j* or *soft g*, and though the Latins hardened it, apparently, into a K value.

The first serious remark is called for on our coming to the change made by both the Greeks and the Latins of the Semitic soft aspirate consonant ı into their vowel E. It would almost seem as though the old Phenicians used that letter as a final vowel, exactly as is done by the Persians and Turks at present. A more remarkable divergency, inexplicable to me, but parallel to the foregoing conversion, is the change made by the Greeks of the Semitic hard aspirate consonant ⌣ into their long vowel H, η, whereas the Latins preserved the letter as a consonant and as their sole aspirate, under the same written form as that used by the Greeks, H, h, and which was in reality the Phenician form of the letter.

The next remark is as to the Latin F, which the Greeks long ago discarded from their alphabet, after having in the first instance adopted it in its Phenician form ⊤, and used it to represent the numeral 6. After discarding it as a letter, they continued to use it as a numeral, though with a corrupted, cursive form, ς, to which they still, to this day, give the Phenician name of Bav, واو, waw, vav. The Latin modification of its sound, from a *w* or *v* to an *f*, is of no importance. The Arabs of to-day, having no *v* letter or sound in their language, write the name of Her Majesty the Queen-Empress, *Fiktoriya*.

As the Greek phonetic value of Z exactly corresponds to the Semitic power of ׃, their numeral value being identical, and the form of the Latin G being merely a modification, one is tempted to imagine that originally the Latin power of this letter was soft *g*, our *j*, perhaps even our *z*. Certain it is that in some dialects of Italian a *z* is used in words where a soft *g* is found in other dialects.

The Greeks made the Semitic ḃ into their Θ ; the Latins, having no such sound, discarded the letter.

The Semitic ی being both a consonant, like our *y*, and also a long vowel, ı, it followed, as a matter of course, that both Greeks and Latins should make it into the vowel *i*. But the Latins preserved its consonantal use also as an initial; though they forgot, or never realized, that it is a consonant in that position. We now use a *y* to express that value; but the Germans have adopted the Latin modification *j* to represent it. Three western letters, ı, *j*, *y*, are now used for the one Semitic ی.

The next four letters require no comment; but the Semitic س of the eastern Arabs is not a good parallel for the Greek Ξ. The Hebrew letter D, that holds its place in the alphabet, is the equivalent of the Arabic ص, and the western Arabs of Morocco transpose the س and ص in their أعجل

alphabet, making the fifth word صعفض, the letter ض being the exact equivalent of the Hebrew צ in place and in power. The ص is a better representative of Σ than the س, but the two sounds are still very remote from one another. I should be inclined to suggest that when the Greek alphabet was formed, the Semitic شِ held the place afterwards taken by the ص and the س. The Greek Σ is an attempt to represent our value *sh*, as is seen in the name Xerxes, of which the old Persian was *Khsharsha*. The Latins dropped this letter, whichever it really was.

The conversion of Semitic consonantal ع into Greek and Latin vowel *o* is not unnatural. This letter ع is absolutely unpronounceable by any other than a Semitic. It is a kind of convulsion in the throat; and as the two aspirates were converted into vowels, so was this guttural. This was so much the more to be expected, as the Semitic letter ا, which became Greek and Latin *a*, is also a guttural consonant, serving likewise as a long vowel on occasions. It is the soft guttural, of which the ع is the hard parallel; and an *o* may well be looked upon as a hard *a*.

What the Arabians use as *f*, ف, is read in Hebrew, as in Greek and Latin, *p*. Even the Arabians, when they have to express a foreign letter, *p*, which they cannot pronounce, write and pronounce it as a *b*, or as *f*. The next letter, ص or ض, is dropped in both Greek and Latin. It appears never to have been used in Greek, even as a numeral; differing in

that respect from the ד. When this latter was dropped as a
letter, it was retained, modified, as a numeral. But the
omitted letter ص became the numeral σαμπι, ϡ representing
900 instead of 90.

From this omission of the ص from its proper place in the
Greek numerals, a slip of the whole subsequent series became
necessary, so that each letter, from ق, Ϙ, Q, onwards, had a
higher numeral value by one degree in the Semitic than its
representative had in Greek; ق standing for 100, while Ϙ
has the value of 90 only; ر represents 200, while P stands
for 100 only; &c. This slip is very remarkable; it was filled
up further on by ϡ 900.

Although the six "additional" letters of the Semitic and
Greek alphabets have no relation to each other as repre-
sentatives of sound, their numerical value goes on exactly
in the same order observed in those of the original series,
and with the same slip up to ڭ, representing 1000, while ϡ
is only 900. On the other hand, however, the three Greek
additionals, υ, φ, χ, are evidently the originals in form of the
Latin u, v, x, and the Semitic ژ is possibly the original of the
Latin Z. This letter is usually attributed, by ancient and
modern authors, to the Greek ζ, which it certainly agrees
with in shape, though not in sound.

The forms of the Arabic and Persian Ottoman letters given
above are those of the isolated characters. They are liable

to various modifications, according to their being initials, medials, or finals, in a combination of written letters.

In the first place, they may, in this respect, be conveniently divided into two classes : those which join on to the following letters in writing a combination, حروف وصلیه hurufu' vwaslíyye, and those which do not so join, حروف ه وصله hurufu munfasílá. The latter, the less numerous class, are : ا, د, ذ, ر, ز, ژ, و and ی; eight in number ; thus, اَبْ, دَتْ, ذَـــْ, رَتْ, زَنْ, ژَاژْ, وَرْ, لَامْ. All the others join, as بَا, بَبْ, بَتْ, یَبْ, تَتْ, نَجّ, جَا, چَبْ, حَبْ, مَجّ, لَجّ, كَثْ, قَتْ, فَبْ, غَبْ, عَا, ظَجّ, طَكْ, ضَتْ, صَبْ, شَبْ, سَا, خَجّ, یَبْ, هَا, نَجّ, &c.

All the letters join on in writing to the character that precedes them (other than to the eight enumerated above) whether they be themselves finals or medials. As finals their forms are as follows : نَا, حَبـ, حَبّ, حت, سَتْ, شْ, صِجْ, ضِجْ, تَغْ, یَعْ, بَظْ, یَطْ, هَضْ, نَصْ, مَشْ, لَسْ, كَثّ, قَزْ, فَرْ, غَذْ, عَدْ, طَخْ, طَلَا, طَ, صَه, ضو, سَ, رَسَمْ, حَا, حَكْ, حَتّ, تَفْ. As medials they are figured thus : نَاب, حَبـ, حَبّ, تَر, سَتَر, شَلَ, بَجِن, مَحَا, اسَ, شَخَبْ.

¹ It having been found impracticable to mark in type the varying Ottoman tone-values of the Arabian and Persian long vowels, the student must learn to supply the numbers 1 and 2 over the long-vowel marks. For this purpose, he must apply the rules for the short vowels, according as they follow, or are followed by, a consonant of the soft or hard class. By practice, the correct habit will be thus acquired ; the case of the short vowels teaching the tone, which will then be instinctively used when the vowel is long.

نَكَظْ , ضَقَلْ , صَفَرْ , ضَغْثْ , بَعْثْ , بَظْرْ , سَطْرْ , خَضْنْ , فَصْلْ , عَشْرْ , طَسْتْ
, كَلَرْ , نَمَرْ , حَنَتْ , حَهَلْ , صِيْنْ . Those which do not join are, as
medials, thus written : باب , هُدَرْ , ذَذل , فَرْطا , جزم , پَرْمَرده , صَوْب , لاز.
Longer combinations vary, *ad infinitum*, as follows : حَرْفَنْ ,

عَدَالَتْ , احْتِجَاجْ , مُتَوَسِّطْ , قَايِلُوْن , مُتَنَاظِرْ , تَجَاهُلْ , كُلْمِيْنْجَه , أُوتُورْمَغْلَه , رَنْجَبَرَلِكْ ,
صِبَعَسْكَرْلِكْ , نَادِ اْ اَنَه , &c.

Besides the simple names of the letters hitherto mentioned,
most of the characters have other, more complicated appel-
lations.

The ا is usually called hemze, هَمْزِه, when a consonant, in an
Arabic word ; and elifi memdude, اَلِفـ مَمْدُوْدَه, *prolonged* ا,
when it is a long vowel, initial or medial. It can never be
a *long final* vowel in an Arabic word, being then always
followed by another consonant hemzè ; as, شَا sha'a, حَزاٌ jeza'u,
&c. It is called elifi maqsure, اَلِفـ مَقْصُورِه, *shortened* ا, when
final. It is then more commonly written ى in classical
Arabic ; but by no means always so. In Persian and Turkish,
or foreign words, the ا is always a vowel, but is called
indifferently elif and hemze. It is always long in Persian
words, when medial or final. When initial in a Persian word,
it may be short or long. When a long initial, it is distinguished, as in Arabic, by the sign medd, مَدّ (ˉ) over it, as :
A. آفَت afet, P. آبـ ab. When a short initial, it is, in Arabic,
generally a consonant, and may take the sound 'a or 'e, of 'l,

or of 'u. When a short initial in Persian, it is a vowel, and
may have any one of the three values a or e, ı, ú. The details
of the powers of ١ in Turkish words are given further on.

The ب is distinguished from the other letters of the same
isolated form by being called بَاءِ مُوَحَّدَه (ba'l muvahhade), *the
single-dotted* ب ; as the ت is named تَاءِ مُثَنَّات (ta'l musnat),
the double-dotted ت, and the ث is designated ثَاءِ مُثَلَّثَه (sa'l mu-
sellese), *the triply-dotted* ث. The ت is further distinguished
from the ط, also named ta, طا, by being called تَاءِ قَرَشَت (ta'l
qarashat), *the* ت *of* (the word) قَرَشَت ; while ط is named
طَاءِ حُطّى (ta'l hútti), *the* ط *of* (the word) حُطّى. Again, the ت
is distinguished, as a medial or initial, from the ى, then identical in form with it, by being called مُثَنَّات فَوقَّه (musnatl fev-
qíyye), *superiorly double-dotted* ; whereas the ى is then
termed مُثَنَّات تَحَتَانَّه (músnatl tahtanlyye), *inferiorly double-
dotted.* The ث is also called ثَاءِ نَخَذ (sa'l sakhaz), *the* ث *of* نَخَذ.
The ب might be called بَاءِ ابْيَجَد (ba'l ebjed), *the* ب *of* ابجد ; but
I do not recollect the expression. It is, however, distinguished from the Persian پ by being designated بَاءِ عَرَبِـَّه (ba'l
'arabîyye), *the Arabian* ب, the پ being called بَاءِ فارِسَـه (ba'l
farîsîyye), and با ءِ عَجَمِـَّه (bā'l 'ájámîyyè), *the Persian* پ.

The simple name of the ج, ـج, ـجـ, جم, sufficiently distinguishes
the letter from all other Arabic characters. It has, therefore,
no other designation in purely Arabic works. It is, however,

distinguished from the Persian ـ by their being styled respectively حيم عَرَبِه (jiml 'areblyye), and حم فارسِه (jiml farlslyye),
or حيم عَجَمِيَّه (jiml 'ajamlyye).

The ـ and خ are distinguished from one another by the
terms حاء مهمله (ha'l muhmele) *neglected* (undotted) ـ, and
خاء مُعْجَمه (kha'l mùjeme) *distinguished* (dotted) ـ, respectively.
In Persian they are often called حاء بِی نُقطه (ha'l bi-nùqta) *dotless*
ـ, and خاء نقطَه‌دار (kha'l nuqtà-dar) *dot-possessing* (dotted) ـ.
These two pairs of Arabic and Persian adjectives go all
through the alphabet, in the cases where a dot is the sole
distinction between two letters of the same form ; as, دال مهمله
(dall mùhmele) د ; ذال مُعْجَمه (zall mùjeme) ذ.   So also the
distinctions by the words of the " numeral alphabet " as,
رَاء قَرَشَت (ra'l
qàràshàt) ر ; زَاء هَوَّز (za'i hèvvèz) ز ; &c.; سِين مهمله (sinl mùh-
mèlè), س ; شِين مُعْجَمه (shinl mù'jèmè), ش ; &c.

When we come to ن, the written names of the letters are
so distinct of themselves, that no addition is necessary for
فا (fa), ف ; قاف (qaf), ق ; كاف (kyaf, *vulgarly* kef), ك ;
لَم (lam), ل ; مِیم (mim), م ; نُون (nun), ن ; وَاو (vwaw), و.
With ه a distinction again comes in, to differentiate the letter
from ـ. We, therefore, say هَاء هوز (ha'l hevvez), ه ; as the
ـ is then termed حاء حطی (ha'l hùtti); and ی is termed, as

mentioned above, باء مُثَنَّاتِ تَحْتَانِه (ya'l musnatl tahtanlyye);
being also called يَاء حُطِّى (ya'l hûttl).

The Persian ب and ـ are distinguished as is described
above; and in like manner the ژ is called زاء فارسِّه (za'l farlslyye), and زاء عَجَمِّ... (za'l 'ajamlyye).

There remains now to distinguish, among consonants, the
different sorts of ك used in Ottoman Turkish, and to point
out their several names, as follows: The original Arabian
ك is named كَف عَرَبِّه (kyafl 'areblyye, vulg. kefl àrebi), the
Arabian ك; its value is that of our k. This letter was next
used by the Persians for their hard g; it was then, and is
still, distinguished by the name of كاف فارسِه (kyafl farlslyye,
vulg. kyafl farlsı, kefl farlsi), and كاف عجمِّه (kyafl 'ajamlyye,
vulg. kefl 'ajaml). This variety is sometimes distinguished, in
writing, in one or the other of two different methods. The
Persians themselves mark the difference by doubling the
upper dash of the letter in all its written variations—isolated,
initial, medial, and final; thus: گ, گل, مگر, سك; whereas the
original Arabian ك, when isolated or final, has no dash at all;
as, ابوك, انك; and a single dash, when initial or medial; thus:
كدر, نكته, also shaped كدر, نكته.

When these two values of the one letter ك passed into use
for the Ottoman language, a new mode of distinguishing the
Persian from the Arabian variety was introduced. It con-

sisted of placing three dots over the Arabian form of the ك, together with a single dash in non-final positions; thus: ك, كُل, مَكُر, سَك; thus marking the Persian *hard g* value of the letter.

But this letter, so differentiated in Persian writing, received in Ottoman Turkish a third value, that of our consonantal *y*, as a softened variety of its Persian value of *hard g*. This Ottoman value never occurs elsewhere than at the end, or in the middle of a word; as: بَك (bèy), بَكنَمَك (beyanmek), يكرمى (yiyirmi), ايرنمَك (iyranmek). In the middle of a word it may begin or end a syllable: be-yan-mek, iy-ran-mek. When this letter follows a *u* vowel, and is itself followed by an *e* vowel, it glides into the value of our *w*; as سوكه (suwè), &c.

In Turkish, the ك, retaining the same form, received another value still, the fourth; being then for distinction's sake, called *surd* ن, صاعِر نون (saghîr nun); as in اَك (èn), آنَمَق (anmaq), سنك (sanin), قونور (qônur). This value is never initial. When medial, it may begin, and may also end a syllable, as it ends many words. The three dots over the ك, mentioned in the preceding paragraph, are used by some to designate this Turkish value of *surd* ن; and at other times a single dot is used for that purpose, leaving the three dots to mark the Persian value of the letter. These varying values of the ‏م‎ constitute a serious difficulty in learning to read Ottoman Turkish. *Surd* ‏ن‎ is here transliterated n.

A similar variation in the phonetic value of the Arabic letter ‏ڭ‎ is to be observed in Ottoman Turkish words. Originally it is, in an Ottoman mouth, a simple hard *g;* as : ‏غالب‎ (galìb), ‏اَغْلَبْ‎ (agleb), ‏مَغْلوبْ‎ (maglub). In Turkish words it has a softened value, very much like that of our *gh,* but still more softened, even to the point of practically disappearing from the pronunciation ; as : ‏طاغْ‎ (dagh, almost daw), ‏طاغِين‎ (daghìn, almost da'ìn), ‏طاغَه‎ (dagha, da'a), ‏طاغی‎ (daghì, da'ì), ‏طاغْدَن‎ (da'dan), ‏طاغْده‎ (da'da), &c. When preceded by an *o* or *u* vowel, the ‏ڭ‎, in Turkish words, if followed by a vowel, glides into the value of our *w,* even as our own *gh* does in the word *throughout* (pronounced *thruwout*) ; as : ‏طوغان‎ (dowan), ‏صوغان‎ (sòwan), ‏قوغش‎ (qowùsh) ; or it nearly disappears in pronunciation, as before ; thus : ‏اُولْدیغِمْ‎ (olduwum, or oldu'um), ‏اُولْدو‎ (òldùwu, or oldu'u).

SECTION II. *The Phonetic Values of the Letters and Vowel-Points, the Uses of the other Orthographic Signs, our System of Transliteration, and the Doctrine of Ottoman Euphony.*

We must divide the thirty-one Ottoman letters (omitting ‏ي‎) into vowels and consonants. But it must first be premised that every letter is sometimes a consonant, while only four of them are sometimes vowels. These are ا , و , ه , ی . All the others, twenty-seven in form, are always consonants. It will be more convenient to treat of the four vowel letters first, together with the vowel-points, which are not letters, but simply marks.

Usually, the vowel-points, three only in number, are not written ; they are supposed to be known. But, in children's books, in Qur'ans, in books of devotion, &c., they are written ; and sometimes in other books and papers also.

The vowel-points are named : 1, ustun, اوستون (over), the mark of which is a short diagonal from the right downwards towards the left, placed *over* any consonant ; as: بَ , تَ , ـَ , &c.; 2, esere, اَسِرہ (no meaning), a similar diagonal, marked *under* any consonant ; as: ـِ , ـِ , دِ , ذِ , &c.; 3, uturu, اوتورو (no meaning), a small و-shaped mark, placed *over* any consonant ; as: سُ , ذُ , زُ , رُ , &c.

These vowel-points mark, originally, the three Arabic short vowels, to which the additional Ottoman vowel-sounds, a, a, a have been added. The ustun has the value of å or e, according to the consonant, &c., accompanying it ; the eseré has the value of í or î ; and the uturu that of ò, u, u, u, also according to its accompaniment.

The short vowel-sound indicated by each of these three marks always follows, in pronunciation, the sound of the consonant to which it is appended ; so that we have the following

Ottoman syllabary, No. 1 : ـبَ ba, ba, ba, ba, bè ; ـبِ bi, bi ;
ـبُ bo, bu, bu, bù ; and so on through the alphabet.

When it is required to make the vowel long, one of the
three Arabic *letters of prolongation*, حَرْفِ مَدّ (harfî medd, *pl.*
حُرُوفِ مَدّ hurufî medd), has to be added to the consonant, still
marked with its short vowel-point. The letters of prolongation, true *long vowels*, are ا, و, ى ; of which ا always accompanies ustun, ى always accompanies eserè ; and و always
accompanies uturu. We now have Ottoman syllabary No. 2,
as follows : بَا ba, ba ; بِى bi, bi ; بُو bo, bu, bu, bū ; &c.

We thus see that there are eleven Ottoman short vowels,
and eight long. Our system of transliterating them is also
made apparent. It is the simple method of using *a* or *e* to
represent ustun, *i* to represent esere, and *o* or *u* to represent
uturu. As these vowel-points shade off in phonetic value, we
use a, a, a, a, or è for ustun ; i or i for esere ; and ò, or u, u,
u, for uturu. After long consideration, we have for some
years past adopted this system, as the simplest, and, on the
whole, the most rational.

The values of these Ottoman vowels are those of the vowels
in the following eleven words. They are all familiar English
words, excepting the French *tu*, the vowel of which is
unknown in ordinary English, though it exists in the dialects
of some of our counties. These words are: *far, war, a-*(bove),

pan, pen ; pin, girl ; so ; put, tu, cur. We mark the vowels
of these eleven guide-words to the Ottoman pronunciation, in
the order in which they stand : far, war, above, pan, pen, pin,
gìrl, sò, put, tu, cur ; and for the eight Ottoman long vowels
we use: far, war, pın, gırl, so, put, tu, cur. That is, nineteen
Ottoman vowel-sounds in all, long and short. The student
has but to remember the series of ten English words and one
French, to become possessed of the key to the Ottoman vowel
pronunciation. But he must learn never to swerve from the
values of those guide-vowels. To an Englishman, with our
slouchy method, this unswervingness is the most difficult
point ; but, with a little patience at first, it is to be achieved.
He must practice himself in pronouncing pasha, باشا (not
pashaw), baba, بابا (not bayba), dan, دَن (not den), san, سَن
(not sen), ben, بَن (which he will at once pronounce right),
ìs-(temek), اِسْتَمَك, fìr-(lamaq), فِرْلَامَـق, qòl, قَوْل (not qal),
qùl, قُول (not qùl), yùz, يُوز (not yùz or yùz), and gyùz, كُوز
(not gyuz or gyuz, though these are also words or syllables).

The English student of Turkish has to exert his utmost
care, in respect of the Ottoman vowels, to break himself of
the home method of pronouncing a short vowel, and the same
vowel when long, in two very different ways. The Ottoman
vowels remain always pure ; they never change in phonetic
value with a change in phonetic *quantity;* thus, a is always á

made long; ī is always ı long, ō is always ŏ long, u is always
ŭ long, &c., in the same word and its derivatives.

The student will have noticed above the Arabic *sign of
quiescence* of a consonant. It is named jezm, جزم and is never
placed over a vowel, long or short.

The fourth Ottoman vowel letter, ه, which, when a consonant, is the soft aspirate *h*, is also derived from the Arabic,
but has a special history of its own. This letter is never
used as a vowel in Arabic in any other position than that of
a final to a noun, substantive or adjective, usually of the
feminine gender, sometimes singular, and sometimes an
irregular (*broken*, technically) plural. Such are the words—
خَلِفَه khalīfe, سُنّه sunne, حَسَنه hasana, طَيِّبه tayyıbe, &c.

In Arabic, these pronunciations (as modified in Ottoman
Turkish, as to the vowels, and as to the consonants) are those
of the words when they close a sentence or clause in classical
reading. They are also the pronunciations of the words in
modern conversational Arabic.

But, originally, and to this day, in classical Arabic, those
and all such words end not in a vowel at all. They all end
in a consonant, in a letter *t* ; which, for certain grammatical
reasons, is never figured ت, but always appears in the shape
of a letter ه surmounted by the two dots of the ت, thus ة.
Our specimen words are therefore, originally, خَلِفَة khalıfet,
سُنّة sunnet, حَسَنة hasânet, طَيِّبة tayyıbet. There are other

vowels and consonants to be added to the termination of these in classical Arabic, to mark the case-endings or declinations. Thus خلفة, when definite, may be marked خلیفتُ khalīfetu for the nominative, خلیفتِ khalīfetī for the genitive, خلیفتَ khalīfetă for the accusative. When indefinite, it becomes خلیفتٌ khalīfetun, خلیفتٍ khalīfetīn, خلیفتً khalīfetan. In all these cases, when final in a sentence or clause, the case-endings are dropped from the pronunciation, though still written in vowel-pointed books, and the word becomes simply khalîfe throughout. These indefinite case-ending marks are called in Turkish ایکی اوتورو (ïkï uturu), *double* uturu, ایکی اسره (ïkï esere), *double* esere, and ایکی اوستون (ïkï ustun) *double* ustun.

A consideration now arose. In classical Arabic, final consonants may be either silent, or vocal with any one of the three short vowels. Thus : کتب ketebet, کتبتُ ketebtu, کتبتَ ketebta, کتبتِ kètèbtī. When such words are final in a sentence or clause, the final consonant is made silent; so that we have ketebet, as before, for the first ; but ketebt for all three of the remaining words. So نصر , نصرَ , نصرُ , final, becomes nasr, as does نصرُ and نصرَ, though نصرً (always distinguished by a servile ا being added—نصرا nasran) remains fully pronounced, or only loses the sound of the final *n*, and is read nasra.

When the final ة of خلفة khalîfe, and similar words, was dropped from the pronunciation, the letter might have been dropped in writing also; for خَايِفْ would read khalife just as well. It could, however, and would, be read حَلِفْ khalif, as Europe has done in making it into *Caliph*. It was necessary, then, to devise a method which should prevent the suppression of the vowel belonging to the last consonant of such words, and yet not be liable to be pronounced as a *t* with the case-endings. This convenient method was discovered by the arrangement adopted of suppressing the dots of the ة, and leaving the nude ه appended to the word, as خَلِفَه khalife, &c. By this method final ه in such words became virtually a vowel in Arabic, though it is never mentioned as such in Arabic grammars or lexicons.

Persian has a very large number of nouns, substantive and adjective, that end in an ustun vowel. When the Arabic alphabet became the sole mode of writing Persian, the Arab teachers would naturally use their quasi-vowel final ه to represent that final Persian sound. Thus, بره bere, سُغْرْنه sugurne, اَمَاده amāde, رِسْده reside, &c., were written. The ه was thus made a vowel in Persian also, when final. It was even made to follow one of the other two short vowels in very rare cases, when no other device was available. Thus we have the numeral سه (sĭ), *three* (in Ottoman Turkish usually pronounced سه se), كه (kĭ), *that*, چه (chĭ), *what, that.*

When, by another historical step, Turkish began to be written in the Arabic characters modified by the special

Persian letters (Turkish scribes learning the method from
Persian teachers in the land of Persia conquered by Turkish
invaders, who there embraced Islam), the use of ه as a final
vowel was found so convenient as to be naturally adopted.
So اه ebe, آده ada, &c., were written. Now, a whole class of
Turkish gerunds, optatives, and imperatives of the third
person, end with this vowel; we, therefore, have اِنْدِه ide,
كِيْدِه gide, كُوره gyúré, قَالَ qálá, قِيْرِه qírá, &c.

A further step was, therefore, possible to be taken in
Ottoman Turkish, from which Persian writers had and have
shrunk. The vowel ه was used as a medial also, whenever it
was found that its introduction served to distinguish two
words written alike, but pronounced differently. Thus بِلْمَك
bilmek, could also be read بِلَّمَك bilemek. If the vowel-points
were always marked, they would suffice for this case; but
they are generally omitted. The gerund and optative بِلَه or
بِلَـه was already in use. By writing بِلْمَك bilmek and بِلَـهمَك
bilemek, the distinction was made clear. Hence, ه as a medial
Ottoman vowel, always indicating a preceding ustun short
vowel-point, became fully established. This medial or final
Turkish vowel ه never joins on to the next letter in writing;
as, اورهمَك uremek, اوطَهده ódaya.

From this sketch of the history of final and medial vowel ه,
we see plainly how fundamentally erroneous is the common

European (or rather English) method of transliterating such words with a final or medial *h*. The nearest approach to correctness of which our orthography is capable, since we possess not the French *e* or German *e*, is to write all such words with a final *a*, as *khalifa*, *Fatima*, *Mekka*, *Medina*, *Brusa*, &c. These are usual ; but جدّه *Jidda*, is usually spelt *Jeddah ;* while قَاهِرِه *Qāhira* (usually *Cairo*), طنجه *Tanja* (usually *Tangiers*), &c., have been made into monstrosities.

The phonetic value of an initial ١ is at first a difficulty to the European student, inasmuch as there appears to be nothing like it in Western languages. This, however, is more apparent than real, when fully explained.

We must remember that in Arabic the initial ١ or أ is a *consonant*, not a vowel. Like any other initial consonant, it takes the three short vowel-points, and is then pronounced: أ ʾe, أ ʾi, أ ʾu. When it became a Persian letter, it was generally named *hemze*, as it is usually called in Arabic when a consonant (but never when a vowel of prolongation, or final and short); although, in Persian words, it is always a vowel, whether initial, medial, or final. With the short vowel-points, this initial ١ is always a short vowel in Persian words, and the Arabian *hemze* sign is never placed over it ; thus : أَ *er*, از ا *ez*, اسب *esb*, است *est*, &c.; اساه *Ispah*, اصفاهان *Isfahan*, &c.; اِلّاغ *ulāg*, &c.

This initial short vowel Persian system was extended (in *practice*, not in *theory*) to all Arabic words used in Persian with ا for their initial letter. But the Arabic consonantal ا was then taken (in practice) to be a Persian vowel ا. Thus, اَبْوَاب was read ebvab, اِبْتِدَا ibtida, اُصُول uṣul; &c.

When, in Arabic, the vowel of the initial consonantal ا became long, then, *as with any other initial consonant*, a vowel letter of prolongation,—a long vowel letter,—was appended to the ا; thus: اَا, pronounced ʼa, اُو, pronounced ʼu, اِی, pronounced ʼi.

This system passed also into use in Persian words, tho Arabic hemzè sign being omitted, even in Arabic words adopted into Persian; and thus the combinations اَا, اُو, اِی, became the initial Persian long vowels; being pronounced respectively—a, u, i. Thus: اَاب ab, اُوبَار ubar, اِیزَد ized; and with words originally Arabic: اَابَا aba, اُوْلَا ula, اِیمَا ima; &c.

The Arabians found the use of اا somewhat cumbersome. They therefore invented a sign, ˜, called medda, مَدَّه, and مَدّ medd, to be placed over an initial ا, with or without the hemzè sign, to designate the long vowel. Thus, instead of اَابَا, they wrote آبَا ʼaba, &c. The Persians adopted this system also, writing آب ab instead of اَاب. The double ا system, however, is still to be found in use in native Persian lexicons; where the first section of chapter ا is generally figured with the two اا, not with آ.

It may be useful to mention here, that the Arabian writers employ this sign of medd to mark a medial or a quasi-final long vowel ١, whenever this is followed in the word by a hemze, ι. e., a consonantal ١. Thus they write تَسَاءلون yetesaʾaluna, حَمْرَاءُ hamrāʾu, &c. These medd signs are omitted in Persian, as well as the final ء; so that حَمْرَا hamra is written, as well as pronounced, for حَمْرَاء; &c.

If a medial consonantal hemzé in an Arabic word be followed by a long vowel ١, the two are united, as in the initial ١, into one ١ letter with the medd sign over it; as مَآل maʾal (for مَأَال). This also is adopted in Persian with such Arabic words as it occurs in; not being found in any original Persian words.

The medd sign is also used, in Arabic, sometimes taking another form, that of a small, perpendicular ١, to mark the traditional omission, in writing (not in pronunciation), of a long vowel ١ in a few well-known words, such as اللّٰه ʾllah (for الٰ), إِلٰهِى ʾllahī (for الاٰهى), رحمٰن or رحمن rahman (for رَحْمَٰن), &c.

This perpendicular small elif-shaped medd is also placed, in Arabic, sometimes over a letter و, to mark that, though radically a و, it is a long vowel ١ in pronunciation, in the two words only, حَيٰوة hayát (usually written حَيَاة, in Persian and Turkish حَات) and صلٰوة salat (usually written صلاة, in Persian and Turkish صَلٰت).

The medd sign is sometimes placed, in Arabic, over a long vowel و or ى, when they are followed by a hemzè in the same word; as in سُوْءُ su'ù, حِىْءَ ji'a. This peculiarity is not used in Persian or Turkish.

It is also sometimes placed over a long vowel medial ا, when this letter is followed by a reduplicated consonant in the same word; as: مَادَّه mādde; it is not used in Persian or Turkish.

Such of the foregoing Arabic usages as have been adopted in Persian for words of Persian or of Arabic origin, are also employed in Ottoman Turkish for the same words; though they are sometimes omitted in ordinary writing.

We now come to a purely Ottoman use of the medd sign, utterly unknown in Arabic and Persian. Thus: Whenever an initial vowel ا of an Ottoman word of Turkish or foreign (European or Indian) origin has the short sound of a or a, the medd sign is placed over it, as a distinction from the initial sounds a, a, e; as: آمِيرَال amiral (French), آرى àri, آطَه ada (Turkish); but اِصَالَتْ asalet, اَوَّل avval (Arabic), اَرْ er (Turkish; also Persian; but two different words).

Another Ottoman peculiarity connected with the initial ا, when followed in writing by a vowel و or ى, is that these two vowels are not *necessarily* long vowels in words of Turkish or foreign origin. Thus اوت ot, اور ur, اوبو utù, اوتْمَكْ utmek, اوفِچ ofichal, ايرْلَانْدَه Irlanda. They may then be called *directing vowels.* In many old or provincial books and writings, these directing vowels are often or systematically omitted, the writers, from habit, or system, adhering to the original Arabic method of spelling by short vowel-points, for the most part omitted in current writing. This makes such books and papers immensely difficult to read and understand.

The three Arabic long vowels, ا, و, ی, having thus acquired a footing as Ottoman short directing-vowels, when following an initial letter ا, it was found convenient to extend the system, and to use them as short directing-vowels, following initial or medial consonants, thereby departing entirely from the Arabic and Persian systems. There is no method in use for distinguishing a long vowel letter from a short one in an Ottoman word of Turkish or foreign origin. We may almost venture to say that all such medial vowel-letters in Turkish and foreign Ottoman words are short vowels; whereas, in Arabic and Persian words they are always long. Thus: ناش bash, قِر qir, مُوش qûsh, اَغْلَامَق aghlamaq, صِزِلْدی sizildi, بُوزُلْمَق bôzŭlmâq, بُوزُلَمَك bŭzŭlmĕk, كُورُلْدی gyŭrŭldŭ, كُورُنَمَك gyŭrŭnmĕk.

Hitherto we have considered only the *open* syllables, that is, those which end with a vowel. We have now to treat of the closed syllables,—those which end with a consonant.

In the original Arabic system, when a word or syllable ended with a *quiescent* consonant,—a consonant not followed by a vowel sound or vowel letter in the same syllable,—such consonant was marked, in pointed writings, by the sign °placed over it, which, as was before remarked, is called jezm, جَزْم . Thus : س beb, ناب bab, بوب bub, سـ bıb, &c.

It is a rule in classical Arabic, that two quiescent consonants cannot follow one another in the same syllable, whether as initials or as finals. Such a word or syllable as *crust, tart, blurt, flirt,* &c., is unknown. As far as two such initial consonants go, this rule prevails in the vernacular Arabic also, and has passed into the Persian and Turkish. Foreign words with such combinations of initial consonants to words or syllables are treated in one of two ways. When initial in a word, they may be separated into two syllables, either by a servile vowel ١, generally with an esere vowel, being prefixed ; or by a vowel, generally esere, being intercalated ; and when the combination is initial to a non-initial syllable of a word, the latter method alone is used, or the syllables are so divided as to separate the two consonants. Thus : κλιμα has become اقليم lqlım, *kral* has become قرال qîral, *prince* has become برنج pîrinj, and *Svizzera* has become اسويچر îsvîchêr.

In classical Arabic, a final word in a phrase or clause could terminate in two quiescent consonants ; as : ربط rabt, علم 'Ilm, حزن huzn, &c. This liberty is much used in Persian, Turkish,

and foreign, as well as in Arabic Ottoman words; thus :
درست durust, اَرْد ard, برس plrlns, برنج plrlnj (*prince*); &c.

When a letter in an Arabic word ends one syllable, and begins the next in the same word, it is not written twice, but one sole letter is made to serve for the two, in pointed writings, by having a special mark, ˝, placed over it. This mark is an abbreviation of the Arabic word شد shedd, which means a *strengthening, corroboration, reduplication.* Thus we have, شدت shlddet, علـة 'lllet, قال baqqal, عطار 'attar, مد medd, ودّ vldd, اـم umm, &c. It is a *sine qua non* in Ottoman reading, and in correct speaking, to redouble such letters in the pronunciation. We can derive a correct idea of this reduplication by studying our expressions, *mid-day, ill-luck, run next,* &c. But, if such reduplicated Arabic word has passed into vernacular Ottoman use, then the redoubling is excused in ordinary conversation; as in the words نَقَّال baqal, عَطَّار âqtâr; &c.

This reduplication is really unknown in Persian; consequently, reduplicated Arabic words are much used in Persian without reduplication; thus خَط is generally used in Persian as خط khat, and has thence, as similar words, passed into Ottoman Turkish. On the other hand, pedantic imitation has commonly given to a few Persian words the Arabic peculiarity of reduplication, so passing into Ottoman also: thus,

بر per (*a wing*), is sometimes pronounced پر perr; and پرنده pėrėndė, پرّنده pėrrėndė; &c.

This reduplicating system is not used in correctly writing Turkish Ottoman words, but it is sometimes met with in incorrect writings. The two letters should be written in full in such Turkish words; thus, چوللق chulluq, بوللـق bȯlluq, اممك ėmmėk, &c.

The Arabic word hemze, همزه, besides being a name for the letter ١, as before explained, is also the name of an orthographic sign, mark, or point, very variously used in Arabic and Persian. Most of the rules concerning it, which derive from the two languages, have passed into Ottoman Turkish, with an addition or two used in the Turkish transliteration of foreign words. Turkish words never require the sign.

The hemze sign, ﺀ, would appear to be a diminutive head of the letter ع, thus indicating to the eye the guttural nature of the vocal enunciation it represents; which is, in fact, a softened choke, in an Arab mouth. But in Persian and Turkish pronunciation it is a slight *hiatus*, at the beginning of a non-initial syllable, or at the end of any syllable, initial, medial or final. It is placed *over* a letter when it bears the ustun or ȕturu vowel, or is quiescent; *under* it, generally, with the esere vowel.

The hemze, in a word of Arabic origin, always represents a consonantal letter ١, sometimes radical, sometimes servile.

In Persian words, the *theory* of the sign is the same as in Arabic, but the sign itself is always servile, and either final or nearly so.

When a hemze, radical or servile, is initial in an Arabic word, it is never written or pronounced in Persian or Turkish. The ا letter is then taken to be a vowel, and is treated accordingly. Thus, اَمَل ᵓemel, becomes اَمَل emel; اِبِْل ᵓibil, becomes اِبِْل ibil; اُمّ ᵓumm, becomes اُمّ ûmm. These are all radicals, and short. So again, اَفْكَار ᵓefkyar, becomes اَفْكَار efkyar; اِقْبَال ᵓiqbal, becomes اِقْبَال iqbal; اُمُور ᵓumur, becomes اُمُور ûmur; &c. These initials are all servile, and short. The modes and doctrine of making them into long vowels have already been described. In Persian, Turkish, and foreign words, an initial ا is always a vowel, and is made long in the same way as if the word were of Arabic origin, as has been said before.

When a hemze, radical or servile, in an Arabic word, is medial or final, a rather numerous body of rules come into play. Sometimes the letter ا, then always called hemze, is written, together with the hemze sign over it, أ (as in رأس reᵓs), and sometimes the hemze sign above is figured, as a letter now, without the ا, in the body of the word; as in يَتَسَاءَلُون yetesaᵓelun. In the former of these two cases, the hemze is usually a final, quiescent consonant in its syllable; as, أَبْت reᵓ-fet, مَأْمِن meᵓ-men, &c. In the latter case, the hemze is the initial consonant of its medial or final syllable, movent with ústún ; as in جُزْءًا juz-ʾán, جَزَاءًا jezáʾán, &c. But it may also be both; that is, a quiescent hemzé may terminate one syllable, while another, a movent hemze, may begin the next syllable. In this case, as with any other consonant so occurring, one ا alone is written, with a hemzé sign over it; and above this, the teshdíd sign is superadded, with an ústún sign over it again; as in تَغَأُّل tefeʾʾel. This step never occurs in Turkish phrases; but the explanation is needed, so as to make clear what follows.

This reduplicated medial hemze, movent with ustún, is sometimes followed by a long vowel ا. In this case, instead of writing, for instance, رَأْأَس, raʾʾas, the two letters ا are combined into one, with the signs medd and hemze, and without the ústún vowel; thus, رَأْس. raʾʾas, as before. This combination is of very rare occurrence, happening only in derivative words, of which the root is triliteral, with hemzé for second radical.

But a movent initial hemzé of a syllable, medial in a word, may be followed by a long vowel ا, without being reduplicated. It is then figured by a single written ا with the hemzé and medd signs; as, مَأَال máʾal, &c.

These combinations, when used in Turkish, drop the hemzé and teshdíd signs, but preserve the medd sign. The ustun vowel that precedes such medd sign is hardened from é into á, on account of the following a, even with a preceding soft consonant.

But, when such medial or final hemze is itself movent with esere, it is no longer written in the form of ا ; it then takes the form of ى, without dots, and with a hemzé sign over it; as, رَئِيس reʾis. If its vowel is uturu, it is written as a و letter, with hemze sign over it; as, رُؤُوس ruʾus. In these two examples the vowels are long; but there are words in Arabic some perchance used in Turkish, in which they are short. Of course, the long vowel letters do not then follow the modified, disguised hemze. Thus, رَائِس raʾis, أَبُؤُس ebʾus.

Moreover, when such medial or final hemze, whether movent or quiescent, is preceded by a consonant movent with esere, the hemzé is figured as a letter ى ; and when movent with uturu, the hemzé is written as a letter و ; in either case surmounted by a hemze sign; thus, بِئْس biʾsa, بُؤُس buʾsa.

Such disguised medial hemzé may be followed by a long vowel letter; as, فؤاد fúʾad, مسؤول mesʾul, رئس reʾis. If the hemze be changed into a ى figure, and be followed by a long vowel ا, it becomes changed in Turkish, and sometimes in Arabic, into a consonant ى ; as in رِيَاسَت riyaset (for رِئاسَت riʾāsét).

There is a striking peculiarity in certain Turkish Ottoman derivatives, which causes great embarrassment to students, and has filled continental Turkish dictionaries and grammars with totally misguiding examples and rules of pronunciation, with regard to the interchangeable vowel-letters و and ى. The peculiarity arose, I imagine, when all Ottoman Turkish was provincial, and was governed by the pronunciation of Asia Minor, variously modified in its various provinces. Thus the earliest writers made use, in all such derivative words, of the vowel-letter و (when they used any at all). They, therefore, wrote گلوب gelub, گیدوب gidub, قاحوب qachub, قیروب qirub, قوروب qurub; and باشلو bashlu, اللو ellu; &c. These derivatives became, in course of time, in Europe, and in Constantinople, modified in pronunciation into gelib, gidib, qachib, qirib, qurub, bashli, elli, &c. The orthography, however, has remained sacred, excepting in the case of provincials, who sometimes write, as they pronounce, قاحـب, گیدیب, گلـب, الّی, باشلی, قریـب, &c. This subject will be further developed in the paragraphs on Euphony.

Proceed we now to the phonetic values of the consonants.

The letter ب, equally used in Ottoman words of Arabic, Persian, Turkish, and foreign origin, has the value of our *b* generally, whether it be initial, medial, or final in a word. Thus: بد bed, بر bir, بار bar, بـز biz, بوز buz, buz, buz, boz; رباط ribāt, ربّط rabt, ثبوت sùbùt; کتاب kitāb, جنوب jènūb, أریب erib, حرب harb, قلب qalb; &c. But when medial or final, ending a syllable or word, it sometimes, anomalously, takes the value of our *p*. Thus it is common to hear, كتاب kìtap, طوب top, اىتدا ìptìdä, كتابچى kìtäpjì. Especially is this the case with the gerunds in وب ; as, گيدوب gìdìp, گلوب géllp, يازوب yàzìp, اوقويوب óqùyùp, قيروب qìrìp.

The Persian letter پ is our *p* in all positions: پدر peder, آپار àpar, ايپ ìp. The Persian word اسپ esp, and the Turkish word طوپ top, are usually written with پ.

The Arabic ت is our *t* in all positions: تاج taj, taj, اتل etel, فتوا fetva, ات et, آت at, ايت ìt, اوت òt. In Turkish grammar it is sometimes changed into movent د in derivatives, when it is originally final and quiescent; as, درت durt, دردنجى durdunjù, دردك durdun, درده durde, دردى durdu, دردم durdum, &c.; ات ìt, ادّر ìder, ايدوب ìdìp, ايديجى ìdìjì ; گيت gìt, گيدر gìder, گيدوب gìdìp, گيديجى gìdìjì ; &c.

The Arabic ث is found in Arabic words only, and in a very few borrowed from the Greek. Its original value is that of our *th* in *think*; so that آياثولوغ àya-thulug, for αγιος θεολογος, was not as bad as our *bishop* for επισκοπος. But in Turkish and Persian this value is unknown; the letter is pronounced as our *s* (sharp, never *z*); aya-sulug is therefore the Turkish name of Ephesus, ثابت is pronounced sàbìt, اثر eser, احداث ìhdàs, &c. In some Arabic-speaking countries this letter has become a *t*; as, ثلاث tàlata, &c.

The Arabic ج in Turkish is our *soft g*, which we represent

by a *j* in all positions of all words, whatever their origin.
Thus, جنس jlns, احناس ejnas, اغا‎ aghaj. In some Arabic-
speaking countries it is pronounced like our *hard g*; as, مسگد
mesgĭd, سگده segda, &c. Sometimes it takes the sharp sound
of چ, q. v.

The Persian چ has the value of our *ch* in *church*, of our *tch*
in *crutch*. We never use the latter orthography in our transliterations,—always the former; as, اچمق achmaq, چام cham,
چورك churĕk, چوروك churŭk, چوربا chŏrbá, ايچ ĭch, چك chĕk,
چچك chĭchek. In Turkish derivation, this letter, in Turkish
or foreign (not Persian, and there are no Arabic) words,
sometimes becomes Arabic ج, but not as a rule.

The Arabic ح has the harshly aspirated sound of our *h* in
horse, hurl, her; not its soft sound, as heard in *head, him, half*,
&c. It is chiefly used in Arabic words; as, حسن hásăn,
حسن huseyn, فتّاح fettah, جرح júrh. We represent it by *h*;
some adopt *ḥ*, to distinguish it from ه, q.v. Aspirate it always.

The Arabic خ has no equivalent in our language. It is the
counterpart of the Scotch and German *ch* in *loch, ich*, &c. It
is generally transliterated *kh*, as in the present treatise. Until
the student has learnt its true pronunciation, he should consider it as a variety of *h*, and never pronounce it as a *k*,
especially when it is initial. Thus خدیو khĭdĭv (pronounce
hĭdĭv, not kĭdĭv), خداوندگار khŭd..vendghyar (pron. hudá...),

ساخ shākh, اخلامور ikhlāmur. In Turkish words, this letter is often used, provincially, for ق, and is itself sometimes pronounced ق. Thus, خالم bakhâlîm (for بقالم baqâlîm), اخشا aqsham (for âkhsham).

The Arabic د is our *d* in all classes of Ottoman words, and requires no comment, unless it be to repeat that, in the derivation of *Turkish* words only, it sometimes takes the place of ت, and is used instead of ط in original words also ; as, كتمك gitmek, كدر gider ; طاغ, داغ dâgh.

The Arabic ذ, in an Ottoman mouth, is a *z*. It is found in Arabic words alone. Different Arab communities pronounce it as our soft *th* in *this*, as a *d*, or as a *z*. The Turk reads, اخذ âkhz, ذكر zikr (*vulg.* zikir), مأخوذ mè-khūz, بذر bèzr.

The Arabic ر is our *r* in every position, in all classes of words : thus, رأفت re-fet, نار bar, ارد ard. There are two important remarks, however, which it is necessary for the English student to bear in mind with respect to this, *to him*, peculiar letter. Firstly, it *must* always be pronounced (never dropped or slurred over, as we pronounce *part*, pa't) ; and secondly, the value of the vowel before it in the same syllable must never be corrupted (as when we pronounce *pot*, pat ; *for*, far ; *cur*, cur ; &c.), but always kept pure, as with any other consonant ; thus, قور qôr, قور qùr, سور sur, كور gyur, &c.; پير pîr, قير qîr, قير qīr ; &c.

The Arabic ز is our *z* in every word and every position; زَادْ zād, زِیرْ zīr, زُورْ zör, زُور zūr, نَزْدْ nezd, اَزْ éz, اَزْ åz, āz, اُوزْ üz; &c.

The Persian ژ is only found in Persian and French words; it is of the value of our *s* in *treasure, pleasure,* and is transliterated *zh*; as, ژازْ zhazh, پِژْمُرْدِه pezhmurde, آتَامَاژُور eta-mazhör, &c. It is of very rare occurrence.

The Arabic س is a soft *s*, always followed by a soft vowel in all words. It must never be pronounced as *z*; thus, اسَا asä, قَوْسْ qåvs, سُوزْ sūz, süz.

The Arabic ش is our *sh*, always; as, شَادْ shad, اِشْ ísh, نَشْرْ néshr.

The Arabic ص, in Turkish, is a hard *s*, used in Turkish, and foreign words also, to designate a hard vowel; thus, اُصّ üss, اَصْمَقْ asmaq, صُوصْمَقْ susmaq, قِصْمَقْ qísmaq. Never read it *z*.

The Arabic ض is very peculiar, being used in Arabic words only. It is generally pronounced as a hard *z* in Turkish, but sometimes as a hard *d*; thus, رَاضِ razí, فَضا qaza, اِنْقَاضْ enqāz; قَاضِی qādí, قَاضِی ٱلْعَسْكَر qāzí-'l-'åskér (vulg. قَاضِی عَسْكَر qåz'-'å-kér), &c. Its Arabic sound is inimitable to a European without long practice.

The Arabic ط, besides being an element of Arabic words, always as a hard *t*, is used in Turkish and foreign words, sometimes with that value, sometimes as a very hard *d*, when initial. Thus, ع ؛ túlú', قُطْر qútr, خ khatt; طولو tatll, طاغ dágh, طوز tuz, طفامق tíqdmáq, طاوْرَانْمَق davranmaq.

The Arabic ظ is used in Arabic words only, as a very hard z. Thus, ظالم zallm, ظلم zúlm, ظفر zffr, ظفر záfer, حَظّ hazz, مَحظُوظ mahzuz.

The Arabic ع is, as a general rule, used in Arabic words only. It is a strong guttural convulsion in an Arab throat, softened in Turkish to a *hiatus*, and often disappearing entirely. We represent it by a Greek *spiritus asper*. Thus, عصر 'asr, طَعْن ta'n, مَلعُون mel un, قطع qat', مقطوع maqtu'. The Turkish word عرب 'arába (for ارابه) is, however, with its derivatives, always written with this letter, of course corruptly.

The Arabic غ is, originally, a peculiar Arabian kind of *hard g*, with a sound vergeing on that of the French r *grasseye*, which English dandies sometimes imitate. But in Turkish pronunciation it is either a simple *hard g*, when initial; as, غالب gallb, غفلت gaflet, غَايْدَه gayda, &c.; and either that when medial or final in Arabic words only, or like our softened *gh* in Turkish words; often disappearing, or nearly so, and changing, like it, into a *w* sound after or before an útúru hard vowel. Thus, اغفال ígfal, صدغ sadg, مغفور magfur; اغلامق aghlamaq, طاغ dágh, أولْدِيغِى olddwú, صوعان sowan, طَوغَان dówan, صُوغُوق sówuq; طَاعُوق tawúq, لاغُوطه láwútá; &c.

The Arabic ف is our *f* in all words and all positions.

There is no reason whatever to write the senseless, false Latin-French *ph* instead of *f*, as in *caliph*, a corruption of khalîfe, خَلِفَه. Thus, فَرْض farz, لَفْظ lafz, صُوفْ sof.

The Arabic ق is our *q* in all words and all positions. It is erroneous and regrettable to represent it by *k*, as is generally done. The words قُرْآن qurʾān, آقْ aq, وَقْت wâqt, are thus correctly rendered, leaving the *k* to represent its legitimate ancestor, ك.

The Arabic ك, in all words and all positions, is our *k*. When initial in a word or syllable before a long ا or و vowel, and also before a short utûru vowel, it borrows, in an Ottoman mouth, the sound of a *y* after itself before the vowel; but not so before the short ustun, the short esere, or the long i vowel. Thus, كَذِبْ kyazlb, أَكُول êkyul, كُوپَك kyûpek ; كَدِى kedl, كَرام khrâm, وَكِيل vekil. Its name, in Arabic, requires no addition; but in Persian and Turkish it has to be distinguished from the Persian letter of the same form, but widely different phonetic value. It is then termed كَافْ عَرَبِّیه kyafl 'areblyye. In Arabic and Persian Ottoman words it remains unchangeable by grammatical inflexion; but in Turkish words, when final, it undergoes phonetic degradation on becoming movent, and is pronounced as a Persian ك, and even as a *y* ; or sometimes as a *w* after an uturu vowel. Thus, اِدَسَك lpêk, اِیَسَكَك lpeylñ, اِسَكَه lpeye, اِیَسَکِى lpeyl ; سُولُوك

súluk, سولوكك suluyuñ, سولوكه suluye, سَوُلُوكَ suluyu; اِيتْمَكْ
İtmek, ايـ كَ ين İtmeyİn.

The Persian ك, called دَفْ فَارِسِّه kyafİ farİsİyye, and
دف فارسی kyafİ farİsİ, or كاف عَجَمِي kyafİ 'ajamı (vulg. عجم دفی
'ajam kafİ), is the Persian *hard g*. It is unknown in Arabic,
is unchangeable in Persian words, and is never final in
Turkish words or syllables. Thus, سَكْ seg, سَكِكْ segİn,
سكه sege, سکی segİ ; گل gal. In ordinary writing and print
it is undistinguished from its Arabic original ; but the Persians
mark it with a double dash : گُل gyul, سَگْ ség. In some
Turkish books it is marked with three dots : کل, سَڭْ.

The Ottoman ڭ, ignored by all previous writers, eastern
and western, consequently nameless, but which we venture
to term كاف عثمانيه kyafİ 'osmanİyye, the Ottoman ڭ, is
found in Turkish words only, as a medial or a final, never
as an initial to a word, though it is used as an initial letter in
a non-initial syllable. Its phonetic value is that of our *y* in
all cases, though it has no mark to distinguish it. It is both
radical, as in دَڭ bey, دكل dİyİl, بِكْرمِی yİyİrmİ ; or it is grammatical, declensional, servile, representing a softened Arabic
radical or servile ك, become movent, as in كُوپَڭ kyupek,
كوپكك kyupeyİn, كُوپَكَه kyupeye, كُوپَكِی kyûpeyİ ; سُورْمَك
surmek, سورمكن surmeyİn ; سودك savdİk, سودبك savdİyİm,
سُودِيكك savdİyİn, سُودَكِی sâvdİyİ. Most European writers

represent this value by *gh ;* but the practice is insufficiently considered, and altogether misleading.

The Ottoman *nasal* ك, distinguished by the name of *surd n,* صاغِر نون saghîr nun, is a second special Turkish phonetic value of the letter ڭ, or nasal letter, which we transliterate with the Spanish nasal n. It has the phonetic value of our English *ng* nasal, as in *sing, thing,* &c. In ordinary writing and print, it has no mark by which a student may recognize it; but sometimes three dots distinguish it, and one recent writer has marked it with one dot, ڭ (as with him the three dots, ڭ, serve to point out the Persian letter or sound). This value is never initial to a word. As a medial, it sometimes ends, sometimes begins a syllable; as, اڭلامق añlamaq (*vulg.* anna-maq), تڭری tañrî (*vulg.* târî); گوڭل gyuñul, دڭز denlz, آڭز añîz, صوڭره sôñrâ (*vulg.* sôra). When final to a word, it is usually sounded as a simple *n;* as, بڭ beñ (ben), سنڭ sanñ (sanln), گلڭ galîñ (gâlîn), طاڭ dañ (dan), صوڭ sôn (sôn). When medially final it is usually softened in like manner, or is elided in pronunciation. In اڭلا مڭ and its derivates (itself derived from آڭ añ), the following ل is exceptionally incorporated with it in pronunciation, as though by a kind of inversion of the Arabic rule of conversion for the ل of the definite article ال before certain letters called *solar* (for which see next paragraph on letter ل).

The Arabic ل is our letter *l* in all words and all positions;

as, وم luzum, ال alîn, دال dal. The Turkish word آكـكلاـمَق,
mentioned above, is, with its derivatives, a modern Ottoman
exception of the capital; and the Arabic rule for the conversion of the ل of the definite article ال, in pronunciation,
when followed by a noun or pronoun beginning with a *solar*
letter, حرف شَمسى harfî shemsı, into that solar letter reduplicated by a teshdîd, is a classical exception, peculiar to Arabic
compounds. The *solar* letters are fourteen in number (exactly
the half of the alphabet); viz., ص ,س ,س ,ز ,ر ,ر ,ذ ,د ,ث ,ت
ص ,ط ,ظ ,ل ,ن . Thus we have الـتِّـين et-tîn, ألـثّـمن es-semen,
es-sûmn, الـدّعَا ed-dâ'ā, ألـدّكـر ez-zikr, ألـسّـمَك es-semek,
esh-shems (whence the name of شمسى), الصّفَا es-safa,
ed-duhâ, ez-zuhâ, الـطّالـع et-tali', الـظّـلم ez-zûlm, اللّاـزِم el-
lazîm, ألـنّـور en-nur. In the pronoun ألّذى, and its derivatives,
the written ل of the article disappears also. The sign ◠ placed
over the ل, so omitted in pronunciation, is named vwasl, وَصْل
junction; and is the letter ص of that word, specially modified.

The Arabic letters م and ن are our *m* and *n* respectively, in
all words and positions: مَال mal, امَل emel, بـن benîm, نَاظِر nazîr,
حزن hûzn.

The Arabic letter و is sometimes a consonant, sometimes a
vowel. When a consonant, it has the phonetic value of our *v*,
of our *w*, or of these two combined, the *v* beginning, and the
w ending the sound of the letter. Thus, وَأر var, حَوَاب jewab,

وصف vwasf, واقع vwaqí'. The ear alone can decide these differences. But when the consonant و is reduplicated in an Arabic word, it has always the *v* value; as, اوّل avval, قوّال qavval. Ottoman corruption even then may sound it, in hard lettered words, as a reduplicated *w*—qawwal. The word قوّاف qawwaf (or قواف qawaf) is an Ottoman corruption of Arabic خفّاف‪‎ khaffaf.

When the letter و is a vowel in an Arabic or Persian word, it always has the value of u; excepting a few Persian words, become Ottoman vernaculars, in which it takes the sound of ó. Thus, لزوم luzum, ممنون memnun; شو shūr; دوست do-t (dust), خوش khosh (khush). In Turkish and foreign words it is generally, if not always, short, and may have either the value of ó, or of u, u, u, which there is no means of distinguishing, save that of accompanying *hard* or *soft* consonants. With a hard consonant, in a Turkish or foreign word, the vowel-letter و (often omitted) must have the sound of either o or u, unless it be considered long, when it becomes ō or u; thus, قومق qomaq, قورمق qurmaq. With a soft consonant, it must be read either u or u, u or u; as, يوزمك yuzmek, سوزلو suzlu. If the accompanying consonant or consonants be neutral, all guidance is lost; as, بوز bóz, buz, buz, سوز suz, suz. In derivatives there is, however, frequently a servile vowel or consonant, hard or soft, that helps. Thus, بوزان bozan, بوزلولق buzlulúq, بوزمك buzmek, سوزمك suzmek; but سوز suz has no such helping derivative. As to the long and short value, each individual ear must decide for itself in words of these two classes—Turkish and foreign. Vowel و is never initial; it must be preceded by ١ to represent an initial uturu sound; as, اولمق olmaq, اولمك ulmek, &c.

The Arabic letter ه has already been fully discussed.

The Arabic letter ى, like the و, is either a consonant or a vowel.

When a consonant, it has the value of our consonant *y*, whether it be initial, medial, or final, simple or reduplicated. Especially must this be understood when the letter is consonantally final in an Arabic word. As a consonant, and only as a consonant, we transliterate it by a *y*. Therefore, when we use a *y* as the final of a transliterated Arabic word, it must be read and sounded as such, never as an *i* vowel; an observation that continental scholars do not generally understand, unless they may be Germans. Thus we have: یر yer, یدك yėdėk, یاز yåz, یوز yůz, بین bėyn, بویون bóyůn; پی pėy, شی shėy, رأی rė‘y, می mėy, حیّ håyy, قیّوم qåyyům, ولّی vėly, رمی remy, وش veshy, مشی meshy. This is a difficulty to a student at first, as we have nothing like it in English.

When the ى is a vowel, it is never initial. If a vowel ı or i sound be initial in any Ottoman word (Arabic, Persian, Turkish, or foreign), the ى, if written, is always preceded by au ا‍‍ ; as, ا‍ل‍د‍ى ldl, اي‍ر‍لا‍م‍ق îrlamaq. When medial, it is always long in Arabic and Persian words; as, ا‍م‍ي‍ر emîr, ب‍ي‍ن bın. In Turkish and foreign words, medial vowel ى is generally, if not always short; as, و‍ي‍ر‍م‍ك vlrmek, ق‍ي‍ر‍م‍ق qîrmaq. When final in an Arabic word, it is also always short; as, ق‍ا‍ض‍ى qāzî, ر‍ا‍ض razî, د‍ا‍ء dā'î, ح‍ا‍ر‍ى jarl, س‍ا‍ر‍ى sarl, &c. But there are hosts of Arabic words ending in reduplicated consonantal ى, which, in Persian and Turkish, are used as Arabic words, generally adjectives, terminating in a long vowel î or î; as, ي‍و‍م‍ى yevmı, س‍ن‍و‍ى senevı, ش‍ه‍ر‍ى shehrı, ع‍ر‍ب‍ى 'arebî, ف‍ا‍ر‍س‍ى farlsî, ق‍ط‍ع qat'ı, ا‍ف‍ق‍ى ůfuqı, ح‍ف‍ظ‍ى hîfzı, &c. When these become feminine, the reduplicated nature of their final consonantal ى becomes apparent; as, ي‍و‍م‍ي‍ه yevmlyye, ق‍ط‍ع‍ي‍ه qat'îyye, &c.

There are many Persian derivative words, adjectives or substantives (besides others not used in Turkish), which really end in long vowel ى. The adjectives are precisely similar to the Arabic adjectives just described, as modified in Persian and Turkish; but they have no feminine. Thus, ش‍ا‍ه‍ى shahı, 'royal;' خ‍س‍ر‍و‍ى khůsrevî, 'imperial;' ش‍ي‍ر‍ا‍ز‍ى shırāzî, 'of Shiraz;' &c. The substantives indicate abstract qualities; as, ش‍ا‍ه‍ى shāhı, 'royalty ;' و‍ز‍ي‍ر‍ى vezîrı, 'vezirial office or functions;' &c.

Turkish and foreign final ى, radical or servile, is always a short vowel; as, ك‍د‍ى kedl, ا‍ر‍ى arî, &c. ; ا‍و‍ى evl, ب‍ا‍ب‍ا‍س‍ى‍ى baba- sını, ا‍و‍ط‍د‍ى ůdayı, ت‍ر‍ه‍ي‍ى tereyl, &c.

The vowels ا and ه are sometimes interchangeable in Turkish words and derivations, and are sometimes omitted, without any inflexible rule being assignable. Thus, اِتْمَامَك, اِتِممَك‎ اِتممدمك, ítmemek, are all admissible. The true rule is: "Never introduce a vowel letter into a Turkish or foreign word without removing a possible doubt as to pronunciation; never leave out a vowel in such word, if by the omission a doubt is created as to pronunciation." The orthography of Arabic and Persian words is fixed, and admits of no such variation. Persian words admit, however, of abbreviation by the omission of a vowel; as, شَاه shah, شَه sheh · پَادْشَاه padshah (*vulg.* pādishāh), پَادْشَه pādsheh; شَاهِنْشَاه shāhinshāh, شَاهِنْشَه shāhinsheh, شَهِنْشَاه shehinshāh, شَهِنْشَه shehinsheh; &c.

In many Turkish words the vowels و and ى are used for one another by different writers, at different times, in different places; even at one place and time; even by one writer at different times, or in the selfsame document; but this last as a license or an inadvertency. Consistency in this matter is advisable. Thus we have: باشلو, bāshlu, باشلى bāshlī, كلُور geldr, كلِر gellr; ارو aru, ارى árí; &c.; words differently written, but the selfsame in reality.

The Ottoman alphabet is divided into three classes of consonants, hard, soft, and neutral. The hard letters are nine in number : ـ, ـ, ص, ض, ط, ظ, ع, ح, ق. The soft letters are only six : أ, ت, ز, س, ك, ه. The remaining letters,

sixteen in the whole, are neutral : ب , ب , ث , ﺚ , ﺩ , ﺫ , ﺩ , ﺭ ,
ﮋ , ﺵ , ﻑ , ﻝ , ﻡ , ﻥ , ﻭ , ﻯ .

As the orthography of every Arabic and Persian Ottoman
word is fixed and unchangeable, it is only in Turkish and
foreign Ottoman words, and in the declensions and conjugations of all Ottoman words, that the rules relating to hard
and soft letters are carried out. This is the first and chief
part of the beautiful system of Ottoman euphony.

If any one of the hard or soft consonants is used in a
Turkish Ottoman word, all the other radical and servile
letters of the word, of its derivations, and of its declension
or conjugation, must be of the same class, or of the neuters.
Thus we have: قازمق qazmaq, گزمك gezmek ; قازديغی qazdîghî,
کزديکی gêzdîyî ; قارلق qârlîq, کوزلك gyûzlûk ; &c.

The Ottoman vowels are also of these three classes. The
hard vowels are : a, a, î, ï, ô, ō, û, u ; eight in all. The soft
vowels also eight : a, e, î, ı, u, u, u, u. The neutral vowels
are a, a, a. These vowels always accompany their own class
of consonants, or the neutrals. The neutral vowels can
accompany any class of consonant. Thus we have : بابا babâ,
انا ana, پاشا pasha, سن san, بن ben, قرمق qîrmaq, کرمك gîrmek,
قومق qômâq, قورمق qûrmâq, کوزتمك gyûzêtmêk, کورمك gyûrmêk.

When in a Turkish Ottoman word a vowel is the dominant
letter, its consonant or consonants being neutrals, the declen-

sion, conjugation, and derivation from that word follow the class to which the dominant vowel belongs; thus, اتْمَق atmaq, آعِرْلِق aghÎrlÎq, اِيْرْلَامَق Îrlamaq, اُومْمَق ummaq, اُوغْرَامَق óghramaq; اَلَمَك elemek, اِنْمَك Îumek, يُوزْمَك yuzmek, اورْمَك urmek.

When an Arabic or Persian word is declined or derived from, in Ottoman Turkish, its last dominant letter or vowel decides whether the declension or derivation shall be made with hard or soft letters and vowels; thus, مربوط merbut, مَرْبُوطْلِق merbutluq; اَمِير emɪr, اَمِيرْلِك emɪrlÎk; آسَان asan, آسَانْلِق asanlÎq; &c.

When the sole dominant vowel of a Turkish Ottoman word, or the last dominant letter or vowel of a Turkish, Arabic, Persian, or foreign Ottoman word, is of the *o* or *u* class, hard or soft, all possible consonants, and all vowels in the declension, conjugation, or derivation therefrom, not only conform to the class of such dominant, but furthermore, all consecutive servile vowels in the derivatives that would otherwise be esere, become úturú, of the class of the dominant; that is, become ú when the dominant is ó or ú, and become u when the dominant is û or ù; thus, اولدى olgun, اولغنلق olgùnlùq, óldù; طُوعِن tutgun, طُوتْغُنْلِق tútgùnlùq, طوتْدى tutdú; سُورُوكْدُرَك surúkdúrmék, سُورُوكْدُرْلْمَك surukdurulmek; سَ , مَك surush-mek, سُو دَ تَك surûshdurmek, سُورُشْدُرْلُمَك surûshdurûlmek; كُورِشْدُرْلُمَك gyúrushmek, كُو نَ دَ كَ. gyurushdurmek, كُورِشْمَك

E

gyurushdurulmek. But if, in such words, an ustun vowel come in by the ordinary course of derivation or conjugation, and be followed by a syllable or syllables with an esere vowel, the influence of the radical dominant uturu is destroyed by such intervention ; as, نوزشمق bozúshmaq, نوزشمقلق bozúsh-maqlíq, بوزشمغن bozushmaghîn ; نورشماک gyurushmek, كورشمكلك gyúrúshméklîk, كورشمكين gyúrúshméyîn.

CHAPTER II.

The Ottoman Accidence or Etymology.

Section L. *The Noun Substantive.*

THERE is no gender. If the female of an animal has not a special name, as, طاوُق (tawúq), *a hen,* قسراق (qîsraq), *a mare,* انك (inek), *a cow,* قانجق (qanjîq), *a bitch,* the female is named, as with us, *a she...,* دِشِ (dishi) ; as, دِشِ اَرسلان (dishi arslan), *a lioness ;* &c. If the female be a girl or woman, she is never named dishi, but is mentioned as قِز (qîz), *maiden,* or قارى (qarî), *matron,* accordingly ; as, قِز خِدمتجى (qîz khîzmetjî), or قِز خِدمتجى (khîzmetjî qîz), *a servant maid, a maidservant ;* قارى اشجى (qarî ashjî), or اشجى قارى (ashjî qarî), *a woman cook, a cook woman.*

There is, really, no declension of nouns in Turkish ; but the prepositions, perhaps eight in number, by some termed *postpositions,* are subjoined to the noun, singular or plural, the plural being always formed by adding the syllable لر (lar, ler) to the singular ; thus :

Nom.	أوق	ôq	(*arrow*),	أوقلر ôqlar (*arrows*).
Gen.	أوقك	ôqun	(*of* —),	أوقلرك oqlaiîn.

Dat.	اوقه óqá	(to —),	اوقلره óqlárá.	
Loc.	اوقده óqdá	(in —),	اوقلرده óqlárdá.	
Acc.	اوقى óqú	(the —),	اوقلرى óqlárí.	
Abl.	اوقدن óqdán	(from —),	اوقلردن óqlárdán.	
Inst.	اوقله óqlá	(with —),	اوقلرله óqlárlá.	
Caus.	اوق ايچون óq íchún	(for —),	اوقلر ايچون óqlár íchún.	

Nom.	او év (house),		اولر évlér (houses).	
Gen.	اوك évlíñ,		اولرك évléríñ.	
Dat.	اوه évé,		اولره évléré.	
Loc.	اوده évdé,		اولرده évlérdé.	
Acc.	اوى évl,		اولرى évlérí.	
Abl.	اودن évdén,		اولردن évlérdén.	
Inst.	اوله évlé,		اولرله évlérlé.	
Caus.	او ايچون év íchún,		اولر ايچون évlér íchún.	

Most Turkish singulars (not all) ending in ت soften this letter into د before a junctional vowel preposition; thus, قورت (qurt), *wolf,* قوردك qurdún, قورده qúrda, قوردى qúrdú; not so before a consonant or separate word; as, قورتله، قورتدن، قورتده، but اتك atín, اوتى otu, &c.

Most, if not all, Turkish singulars, of more than one syllable, ending in ق, soften it into غ before junctional vowels; as, چارداق (chardaq), *trellis,* چارداغك chardaghín,

داعه chardagha, داعى, chardaghî. Those in Arabic ك soften it into Turkish ك (*y* value); ايپَك (îpėk), *silk*, اسَكك (îpeyîn), اسَكه (îpėyė), ايپلى (îpėyî). Those in Persian ك (*g* value), do not change it; as, سَنَك seng, *stone*, سنگك (sengîn), سَنَكه (sėngė), سَنَكى (sėngî).

These rules do not apply to Arabic and Persian substantives; these retain their final ى or ك unchanged; unless the borrowed word has passed into the mouth of the vulgar as an everyday expression; as, مستق fîstîq, فستغك fîstîghîn, &c.

Singulars ending in a vowel, take ن in the genitive, and consonant ى in the dative and accusative, to support the vowel taken by a final consonant; as, بابا (baba), *father*, بابانك (babauîn), بابه (babayå), بابايى (babayî); قو (qapů), *door, gate*, قپونك (qapůnůn), قويه (qapuya), قويى (qapůyu, where ůtůrů dominates); ارى (arî), *bee*, آرينك (arînîn), آرىه (arîya, written separately on account of two letters ى), اريبى (arîyî); بدى (kedî), *cat*, كدينك (kėdînîñ), كدىيه (kedîye), كدىبى (kedîyî), &c.

Singulars ending in vowel ه do not join this letter to the sign of the plural, in writing; as, پده (pîde), بيدهلَر (pîdeler).

The word صو (sů), *water*, irregularly forms its genitive as صويك (suyůn, almost the only exception or irregularity in the language). صوى (sôy), *sort*, ends in a consonant, and is regular; صويك (sôyun), صويَه (soya), صويى (sôyů).

Arabic and Persian substantives never change their final
consonants for declension; طَبَق (tabaq), *plate*, طَبَقك tabaqın;
اِمْسَاك (imsak), *refraining*, اِمْسَاكـﻪ (imsake); صَلَات (sålat),
worship, صَلَاتِ (salatî).   Their final vowels follow the same
rules with those in Turkish words; دُعَا (du'a), *prayer*, دُعَانك
du'anın); بِيَاده (pîyāde), *foot-man*, بِيَادهیه (pîyadeye); چَارْسُو
charsu), *market*, جَارْسُویی (charsuyu); ثُلَاثِی (sulasī), *triliteral
root*, ثُلَاثِییِی (sulasîyî).

They form their plurals as Turkish words; but Persian
names of men and their kinds use the Persian plural also,
if judged proper. This is formed by adding an ustun vowel,
followed by اِن, to the final consonant of the singular; as,
مَرْد (merd), *man*, مَرْدَان (merdan).   If the singular ends in ﻪ
vowel, it is changed into consonant اِ (Persian), with ustun
vowel, before the اِن of the plural; as, خَواجه (kh'āje), *master*,
خَواجکان (kh'ajegyan).   Singulars ending in vowel و take consonant ی instead of اِ; as, خُوبْرو (khub-ru), *a beauty in face*,
خُوبْرویَان (khub-ruyan).   Those ending in vowel ی change it
into consonant ی in like manner; as, سِپَاهِی (sîpahı), *man-at-
arms*, سِپَاهِیَان (sîpahîyan).   [Persian writers explain this by
saying: "The final long vowel is in reality two letters ی
rolled into one.   One of these is now used as a consonant."]
Other Persian substantives form the plural by adding the
syllable هَا hā; as, نَانْهَا (nān-ha), *loaves*, *breads*, اِسبْهَا (esb-hā),
horses.

Arabic plurals, of the regular forms for men and women, and of the various irregular forms for these and other things, and also the Arabic duals, are used in Turkish. The dual is formed by adding ustun followed by ان (an) in the nominative, which becomes ین (eyn) in the oblique case. The latter is frequently used in Turkish as a nominative; as, قطب (qutb), pole, قطبان (qûtban), قطبین (qûtbeyn), *the two poles.*

The regular plural masculine nominative for *men* is formed by adding uturu followed by ون (un) to the singular. This becomes eseré followed by ین (in) in the oblique case, also used as a nominative in Turkish; the plural feminine is with ûstun followed by ات (at) in all cases; thus, مسلم (muslim), a *Muslim,* مسلمون (muslimun), مسلمین (muslimin), مسلمات (mûslimat), *Muslims.*

The irregular Arabic plurals commonly used in Turkish are of rather numerous forms, and there are many more plural forms used occasionally. These irregular plural Arabic forms are not obtained by adding a letter or letters, vowel or consonant, to the end of the singular, but by varying the vowel or vowels of the word, and by adding letters, consonant or vowel, as the case may be, before, between, or after, the letters of the singular. To enable the student to obtain a fair insight into this very intricate but beautiful system, I have to say, first of all, that a paradigm has been adopted by Arabian grammarians, according to which all such modifications may be effected. They have taken the triliteral فَعَل (fa‘ala) as the representative of any and every triliteral root-word, and they have modified this root into every shape that can, under any circumstances, be taken by any derivative of any triliteral root in the language. All those modifications, when not made on the vowels alone of the triliteral, are effected by adding *servile letters*, or *a servile letter*, here and there, before, after, and in the midst of, the three radical consonants, with appropriate mutations, in each case, of the vowels, long or short, in the new word. Thus, to speak only of Arabic nouns, substantive or adjective, used in Turkish, we have, in the first place, to learn the *forms* of their singulars (for they all have definite forms), and then the forms of the plurals special to each of these singulars.

To facilitate and systematize this knowledge, the Arabian grammarians have divided the whole language into sections of biliteral, triliteral, quadriliteral, quinqueliteral, &c., roots, which they term, respectively, ثُنَائِي (suna’i), ثُلَاثِی (sulasi), رُبَاعِی (ruba‘i), خُمَاسِی (khumasi), سُدَاسِی (sudasi), &c. These are the Turkish pronunciations of the terms. I do not remember ever to have seen or heard the expression أُحَادِی (uhadi), which would be the analogous name for uniliteral root; but it may perhaps be found. Of these, the triliterals form by very far the most important and numerous class, the quadriliterals coming next. These are represented,

respectively, by the supposititious paradigmatic words فَعَلَ
(fa'ala) and فَعْلَل (fa'lele).

Every triliteral root is theoretically capable of giving rise
to fifteen chapters of derivation, called بَاب (bab, pl. أَبْوَاب
ebvab). These chapters are respectively termed : 1, فعل نَابِ
(fa'alâ babî), *the chapter of the triliteral* · 2, تَنْعِلْ بَابِى (tef'îl
babî), *the chapter of* (the verbal noun) تفعِيل ; 3, مَفَاعِلِه نَابِى
(mufa'ale babî); 4, اِنْعَال نَابِى (îf al babî) ; 5, تَفَعُّل بَابِى (tefa''ul —);
6, اِنْعَال نَابِى تفَاعُل نَابِى (tefa'ul —); 7, اِنْفِعَال بَابِى (înfî'al —); 8,
(îftî al —); 9, اِفْعِلَال بَابِى (îf'îlal —); 10, اِسْتِفْعَال نَابِى (îstîf al —);
11, اِفْعِوَّال نَابِى اِفْعَعَال نَابِى (îf'îlal —); 12, اِفْعَعَال بَابِى (îf'î al —); 13,
(îf'îvval —); 14, اِفْعِنْلَال نَابِى (îf'înlal —); 15, اِفْعِنْلَى بَابِى (îf'înla—).
The use of words from the last four chapters is next to
unknown in Turkish, if not quite so ; and the use of chapters
9 and 11, اِفْعِلَال , اِفْعِلَال, is confined to the expression of
colours, the second expressing an *intensity of degree.* All the
other nine chapters of derivation are constantly met with in
Turkish, as nouns, substantive and adjective. Occasionally,
even a verb is used ; but as a kind of invocatory interjection.
All but the first of these names (which is the form of three
out of the six varieties of its verb) is the form of one of the
verbal nouns, or of the sole verbal noun, connected with the
verb of the chapter ; and each chapter has two adjectives

deriving from it, the active and passive participles of the verb of the chapter. The first, or triliteral, chapter possesses, furthermore, several other special forms of nouns deriving from its verb other than its verbal nouns (which are a kind of infinitive, or noun of action or being, corresponding with our English substantive form in -*ing*, as, *walking, singing, cutting, suffering, lasting*, &c., as acts or states). Of these, I give here merely those frequently met with in Turkish ; and it must be understood, that in this simple triliteral chapter, the various forms of verbal nouns are never all found deriving from one verb ; but certain forms belong to one or more kinds of triliteral verbs, others to other kinds. These *kinds* of verbs, again, are of two sorts ; there are verbs transitive or active, and there are verbs intransitive or neuter ; and certain verbal nouns are more used than others with each of these two kinds. Again, there are the six conjugations of this simple triliteral chapter ; and each conjugation has its preferential form or forms of verbal noun. The Turkish Qamus dictionary dilates on this subject more than other works, and much information can be obtained from it, in addition to what should be studied in the " Grammar of the Arabic Language," by Dr. Wm. Wright, vol. i., p. 109, par. 196, where 36 forms of " *nomina verbi* " are given for this triliteral chapter alone, and several others may be found in De Sacy's " Grammaire Arabe," 2nd edition, 1831, vol. i., p. 283, par. 628. Those that are principally used in Turkish are the following: 1, فَعْل (fa'l); 2, فَعَل (fa'ăl); 3, فِعْل (fĭ'l); 4, فُعْل (fŭ'l); their feminines: 5, فَعْلَـه (fa'le); 6, فَعَلَه (fa'ale); 7, فِعْلَه (fĭ'le); 8, فُعْلَه (fŭ'le); the same forms, with an insititious or servile long vowel ۱: 9, فَعَال (fa'āl); 10, فعال (fĭ al); 11, فعال (fu'al); and their feminines: 12, فَعَالَه (fa'ale); 13, فعاله (fĭ ale); 14, فعاله (fŭ ale); some of the same, with long vowel و or ى; and their feminines: 15, فَعُول (fă'ul); 16, فُعُول (fu ul); 17, فَعِيل (fă'il); 18, فَعُولَه (fă ule); 19, فُعُولَه (fu'ule); 20, فَعِلَه (fă'ile); the same, with final servile ان added: 21, فَعْلَان (fa'lan); 22, فِعْلَان (fĭ'lan); 23, فُعْلَان (fŭ'lan); the special feminine form: 24, فعالِت (fă'allyet); and the special forms in initial servile م, with their feminines: 25, مَفْعَل (mef'al); 26, مَفْعِل (mef'ĭl); 27, مَفْعَلَه (mef'ăle); 28, مفعله (mef'ĭle); with the two special forms in initial servile ت, with long vowel ۱ intercalated: 29, تَفْعَال (tef al); 30, تفعال (tĭf al). Many original substantives and adjectives are of one or other of the forms here given; and in frequent cases it is disputed whether such words are substantives or verbal nouns. The active participle, *nomen agentis*, of this chapter is: 31, فَاعِل (ta'ĭl); 32, feminine, فاعِلَـه (fa'lle); and the passive participle, *nomen patientis*, is: 33, مفعُول (mef ul); 34, feminine, مَفعُولَه (mef'ule); derivative adjectives are met with, branches of this chapter, as: 35, فَعِّل (fa'l); 36, فعِل (fă'ĭl); 37, فَعُول (fă'ul; often feminine); 38, فَعِل (fă'il); and the feminine of this last. 39, فَلَ (fa'ĭle);

the diminutive, substantive or adjective: 40, فُعَيْل (fú‘ayl); the noun of unity: 41, فعله (fa‘le); the noun of kind or manner: 42, فِعْله (fi‘le); the noun of place and time: 43, مَفْعَل mef‘al; sometimes mef‘îl and مفعله mef‘ale); the noun of the place of abundance: 44, مفعله (mef‘ale); the noun of instrument and receptacle: 45, مِفْعَل (mif‘al; sometimes مِفعَال mif‘al, and مفعله mif‘alè; rarely مُفْعَل muf‘ál and مفعله muf‘ùle); and others still which need not be classified here, though a knowledge of their special forms and meanings, when acquired, assists greatly to an accurate appreciation of Arabic diction, as occasionally met with in Turkish.

The irregular plurals of these forms mostly met with, when the words are substantives and masculine, are: 1, أفعَال (ef‘al); 2, فُعُول (fu ul); 3, فِعَال (fi‘al); 4, أفْعُل (ef‘ul); 5, أفْعِله (ef‘île); 6, فُعَّال (fu‘‘al) and 7, فَعَلَة (fa‘álè; both for the form فاعل); 8, فُعَلَا (fu‘álâ) and 9, أفعِلا (ef‘îla; both for the form فعِيل fa‘îl); 10, فَعْلَا (fa‘ala; for the form فَعْلَا fa‘la); when they are feminine in form, either; 11, فعَل (fi‘al; for the form فعله fi‘le), or 12, فُعَل (fu‘âl; for the form فُعله fu‘le), or 13, أفْعَال (ef‘al; as for masculines); 14, فعائِل (fa‘a>îl; for the forms فعاله fa ale, فَعُوله fa‘ule فاعِله fâ‘ile); 15, فواعِل (feva îl; for the form فَاعِلَة); besides 16, مَفاعِل (mefa îl; for the forms mef‘al, mef‘îl, mif‘al, and their variants); 17, مفاعِل (mefa îl; for the forms مفعال, مَفعُول); and others more rarely used.

Adjectives masculine derived from this triliteral chapter, much used in Turkish, are of the two forms فَعِل (faïl) and أَفْعَل (efal); feminines, respectively, فَعِلَه (faïle) and فَعْلَا (fa'la, for Arabic فَعْلَاءُ; of افعل when not comparative) or فُعْلَا (fu'la, for Arabic فُعْلَى; of the same افعل when comparative). The plurals of these are: فعلا (fu'ala) or أَفْعِلَه (efïle), for فَعِيل, as in the substantive; and فِعَل (fïl), for أَفْعَل and its feminines.

We now come to the derived chapters.

The verbal nouns of the second chapter are: تَفْعِيل (tef'ïl), تَفْعَال (tef'al; sometimes tîf'al), and تَفْعِلَه (tef'île); the plurals of the whole of which are of the form تَعَاعِيل (tefa'ïl); though the first makes also a quasi-regular plural, تَفْعِيلَات (tef'ï'at). Its active participle is مُفَعِّل (mufa''ïl, fem. مُفَعِّلَه mufa'île); and its passive participle is مفعّل (mufa''al, fem. مُفَعِّلَه mufa''ale), of which the masculine is also used as a noun of time and place.

The verbal nouns of the third chapter are: مُفَاعَلَه (mufa'ale) and فِعَال (fï'al; this latter only occasionally used); the active participle is مُفَاعِل (mufa'ïl, fem. مُفَاعِلَه mufa'île); the passive participle, مُفَاعَل (mufa'al, fem. مُفَاعَلَه mufa'ale, exactly like the first verbal noun).

The verbal noun of the fourth chapter is إِفْعَال (ïf'al); a. p. مُفْعِل (muf'ïl, fem. مُفْعِلَه); p. p. مُفْعَل (muf'al, fem. مُفْعَلَه).

The fifth chapter has: *v. n.*, تَفَعُّل (tefa"úl); *a. p.* مُتَفَعِّل (mute-fâ"íl, fem. مُتَفَعِّلة); *p. p.* مُتَفَعَّل (mûtefâ"al, fem. مُتَفَعَّلة).

The sixth : *v. n.* تَفَاعُل (tefa'úl) ; مُتَفَاعِل (mûtefâ'íl, مُتَفَاعِلة); مُتَفَاعَل (mûtefaʼal, مُتَفَاعَلة).

The seventh : اِنْفِعَال (ínfîʼal), مُنْفَعِل (mûnfaʼíl, مُنْفَعِلة), مُنْفَعَل (mûnfa'al, مُنْفَعَلة).

The eighth : اِفْتِعَال (íftîʼal), مُفْتَعِل (mûftaʼíl, مُفْتَعِلة), مُفْتَعَل (mûf-tâʼâl, مُفْتَعَلة).

The ninth: اِفْعِلَال (ífʼílal), *a. p.* مُفْعَلّ (mûfʼâll, مُفْعَلّة mûfʼalle); no *p. p.*

The tenth: اِسْتِفْعَال (ístîfʼal), مُسْتَفْعِل (mûstefʼíl, مُسْتَفْعِلة), مُسْتَفْعَل (mûstefʼal, مُسْتَفْعَلة).

The eleventh: اِفْعِيلَال (ífʼílal), مُفْعَالّ (mufʼâll, مُفْعَالّة mûfʼâllé) ; no *p. p.*

As to the significations of these chapters, it may be shortly said that when the first is transitive, the second is causative or intensive ; and when the first is intransitive, the second—causative still in the same sense, but not intensive—is transitive. Sometimes the second has the sense, not of making (a thing) do or be (so or so), but of making (it) out to be (so and so), of deeming, judging, pronouncing, or calling (it so and so) ; rarely, it unmakes also.

The third chapter denotes reciprocity of the action between

two, or among several or many agents, or an expected reciprocity when one agent only is shown. Thus, مُكَاتَبَة *a mutually writing letters* (to one another), *a writing in expectation of a reply;* قَاتَل *a mutually striving to kill one another, fighting.* When the triliteral is expressive of a state, as حُسْن (husn), *a being beautiful or good,* the third form expresses an action corresponding with that state in the agent; thus, مُحَاسَنَة (muhasene), *a doing good, and acting well, kindly to* (the other).

The fourth form is causative, generally, but sometimes intransitive; thus, اِرْسَال (irsal), *a sending* (some person or thing); اِقْبَال (iqbal), *an advancing.*

The fifth form has the sense of acquiring a state, sometimes by one's own act, sometimes through the act of another; as, تَكَسُّر (tekessúr), *a becoming broken.* This may be transitive at times; as, تَعَلُّم (ta'allum), *a becoming knowing in* (a science, art, &c.); i.e., *a learning* (it).

The sixth form has the idea of reciprocity, something like the third, but more decided, more certain in fact; thus, تَقَاتُل (taqatúl), *a mutually killing one another.* Sometimes it has the sense of feigning a state; as, تَجَاهُل (tejahul), *a feigning to be ignorant.* Sometimes, again, it expresses a repeated act; thus, تَقَاضَا (taqaza), *a dunning, repeatedly demanding the fulfilment and discharge* (of some incumbent act or debt).

The seventh and eighth forms, like the fifth, imply the acquisition of a state, either by one's own act, or as the result of the act of another; thus, اِنْفِعَال (Inff'al), *a being acted upon, affected, hurt, wounded, vexed* (by another's act); اِنْتِظار (Intizar) *a* (becoming) *looking forward* (for the occurrence of an event). Sometimes the eighth form is transitive in the sense of *acquiring;* thus, اِفْتِرَاس (Iftiras), *an acquiring* (game) *by hunting;* or, a seeking to acquire; as, اِلْتِمَاس (Iltimās), *a seeking to obtain* (a favour) *by* (morally) *feeling one's way* (by touching, groping, requesting); *a requesting.*

The ninth and eleventh express two degrees of state as to colour, and sometimes as to defects; the eleventh denoting intensity of that state; thus, اِحْمِرَار (Ihmirar), *a being red; redness;* اِحْمِيرار (Ihmirar), *a being very red;* اِعْوِجاج (I'vijaj, *a being crooked; crookedness;* اِعِوِحاـ (I'vijaj), *a being very crooked; anfractuosity.*

The tenth usually expresses *a trying to get* (the act or state signified by the first form); as, اِسْتِفْسار (Istifsar), *an asking for an explanation of* (a matter). Sometimes it has, like the second, the sense of *deeming* or *judging* (a thing) *to be* (what the first form signifies); as, اِسْتِثْقال (Istisqal), *a deeming* (a person or thing) *heavy, disagreeable, tedious.* And sometimes it means *an acquiring a state,* expressed by the first form; thus, اِسْتِشْفَا (Istishfa), *a becoming restored to health.* And again, it occasionally has the sense of the first form ; as, اِسْتِعْدَاد (istl'dad), *a being or becoming ready prepared ; readiness* (external or mental); *mental capacity and quickness in acquiring dexterity or knowledge.*

Quadriliteral roots have but four forms ; of which only two are perceptibly used in Turkish, the first and second. The first has two verbal nouns, figured paradigmatically by فَعْلَلَه (fa'lele), and فِعْلَال (fl'lal) ; the second, but one, figured by تَفَعْلُل (tefa'lul) ; سَلْطَنَتْ (saltanat) may serve as an instance of a verbal noun of the first form, and تَسَلْطُن (tesaltun) as an example of the second.

It would occupy too much space to detail here the modifications of these results arising in the case of roots where the second and third radicals are identical, or of those in which one, two, or all three of the radicals belong to the trio ا, و, ى, out of which the long vowels, the *letters of prolongation,* spring. These details should be studied in Wright's, or in De Sacy's Arabic Grammar. But it is necessary to remark that these Arabic verbal nouns belong equally to the active and passive voice of their verbs; so that, as in English, the same word, فَتْح fet-h for instance, will sometimes mean a *con-quering,* at others a *being conquered,* just as our word *conquest* does. This last rule holds good with Persian verbal nouns, not much used in Turkish. It is not so, however, with Turkish verbal nouns, excepting, to a slight extent, with the present, as in مه ma, me ; and this for the simple reason that every passive Turkish verb has its own special verbal nouns complete, present, past, and future.

Every Turkish, Persian, and Arabic substantive has its diminutive, the two latter seldom used in Ottoman phrases.

The Turkish diminutive substantive is formed usually by suffixing the syllable جِك (jìk) or جِقْ (jìq) to the word, of whatever origin, whether it end in a consonant or vowel. Thus, اِرِكْجِك (erìkjìk) *a little plum,* اِتْجِك (ìtjìk) *a little dog,* كِتابْجِك (kìtabjìk or كِتابْجِقْ kìtabjìq) *a little book,* كاتِبْجِك (kyatlb-jìk) *a little clerk,'* دَوَهْجِك (devejìk) *a little camel,* اوتوجُك (utujuk), *a little flat-iron,* كَدِجِك (kedìjìk) *a little cat,* اَلْماجِقْ (elmajìq) *a little apple,* باشاجِقْ (pashajìq) *a little pasha,* بادِشاهْجِقْ (padì-shahjìq) *a little monarch,* قپوجِقْ (qápùjùq) *a little door or gate,* خواجهْجِقْ (khojajìq) *a little professor,* قاریجِقْ (qarìjìq) *a little woman.*

In words ending with ك or ق, after a movent consonant, it would form a cacophony to repeat these letters for the diminutive. The less important is therefore sacrificed to euphony, and omitted in the diminutive, a vowel letter usually taking its place: كُورك (kyurek), كُورهْجِك (kyurejìk), *a little shovel or oar;* حوجق (chojuq), حوجوجق (chojujuq), *a little child.*

This form of the diminutive is sometimes modified into that of جَكْز (jèylz), جَغْز (jaghìz); thus, اَوْجَكِز (èvjeylz) *a little house,*

قِـزجغـز (qîzjaghîz), *a little girl*. As is seen, the former esere vowel of the ـ in the diminutive has now become an ustun, as the esere has been passed on to the ﻯ or ﻕ, modified into Turkish ﻙ (*y* value) or ﻍ (soft *gh* value). Euphony requires it.

These diminutives are used as terms of endearment also, exactly as in German, and as our nursery vocabulary says, *daddy, mammy, granny, aunty, doggy, horsey,* &c. ; only, in Turkish, the method is of universal application, by all classes, not by children only.

The Persian diminutive always ends in ﭼﻪ (che); as, ﭘﺎ (pa), ﭘﺎﭼﻪ (pache), or in ﻙ preceded by an ustun vowel; as, ﻛﻨﻴﺰ (kênîz), ﻛﻨﻴﺰﻙ (kênîzêk).

The Arabic diminutive also makes its first vowel uturû, and the next vowel ustun, followed by a quiescent consonantal ﻯ, whatever may be the vowels or quiescences of the original word; as, ﺣَﺴَﻦْ (hasan), ﺣُﺴَﻦ (huseyn) ; ﺣﺼﻦ (hîsn), ﺣﺼﻴﻦ (hùsâyn); &c.

The Persian and Arabic diminutive applies equally to substantives and adjectives. The Arabic rule has many modifications in details. But as these Persian and Arabic diminutives are taken into Ottoman use as original words, enough has been said on their subject for the present purpose.

SECTION II. *The Noun Adjective.*

As a general rule, the adjective, in Turkish, is invariable, having no gender, number, case, or degrees of comparison; and this, whether the word be of Turkish, Arabic, or Persian origin. It always precedes the substantive qualified; as, آدَم بُوك (bîyuk adam), *a great man,* بُوك آدَمَلَر (bîyuk adamlar), *great men;* بوك انَـكَّر (bîyuk înekler), *big cows.*

But the Persian form of phrase is also much used (especially in writing), by which an adjective of Persian or Arabic origin follows the substantive qualified; such adjective remaining in the singular after a Persian substantive plural, the substantive qualified always taking an esere of subjection to join it to the adjective; thus, مَردانِ بُزْرَك (merdanî bûzurg), *great men ·* عَمَلْهایِ نِك ('amelhayî nîk), *good works.*

If, in this Persian construction, both words are Arabic, and the substantive is a feminine singular, or an irregular plural of any kind, the adjective must be put in the feminine singular, or in an irregular plural form; as, عَساكِر مُنْتَظِمه ('âsakîrî muntazîme), *regular troops,* سَلاطِیـرِ عِظَام (selatînî 'izam), *great Sultans.*

Persian adjectives have three degrees of comparison, more or less in use in Turkish composition. The comparative is formed by adding the syllable تَر (ter) to the end of the positive; and the superlative, by adding the syllables ترين (terīn); but these never qualify preceding substantives, being only used as substantive members of phrases, or to qualify a following substantive; thus, بهترين وسائل نجات (bihterīnl vesa-'ill nejat), *the best of the means of salvation*; (bihterin vesa'ill nejat), *the best means of salvation.*

Arabic adjectives have but two degrees of comparison. Whatever the form of the positive, the comparative is of the form افعَل (ef'al). This is used, in Persian construction, more as an exaggeration than as a degree of comparison, more as a substantive than an adjective. If followed by a substantive singular, it is a superlative with the sense of *very, extremely, exceedingly*, and the like; thus, أحسَن وسله نجات (ahsanl vesile'l nejat), *a very good means of salvation.* If the following sub-stantive be in the plural, the adjective is a superlative, with the sense of *the most*......; as, احسن وسائل نجات (ahsanl vesa'ill nejāt), *the best of the means of salvation.*

If an adjective be used as a substantive, it admits the plural and the prepositions, as substantives; thus, اولر (iyuler), *the good;* اولرك (iyulerln), *of the good*, &c., &c.

Every Turkish adjective, besides its positive signification, betokens, on occasions, the comparative, the superlative, and an excess of the quality it expresses, which we explain by employing the adverb *too* before the word. Thus, بيوك (bīyuk),

large, larger, largest, too large ; صیجاق (sijåq), *hot, hotter, hottest,*
too hot ; صوعرق (soghůq), *cold, colder, coldest, too cold ;* &c.

The Persian compound adjective, much used in Turkish, in
the positive degree only, is of many kinds. Some are com-
pounded of two substantives, one or both of which may be
Arabic or Persian, never Turkish ; as, حم حناب (jem-jenab),
majestic as Jemshıd ; اصَف تدبیر (asaf-tedbır), *Asaph in counsel ;*
شَکَرلَب (sheker-leb), *sugar-lipped ;* عدالَنت دَسْتْـگاه ('adalet-
destgyah), *a very loom of justice* (i. e., *just*) ; others of an
adjective followed by a substantive ; as, سبـکـای (sebůk-pay),
light of foot, light-footed ; or a substantive followed by an
adjective ; as, دلتشنه (dıl-tıshne), *thirsty-hearted* (i. e., *ardently
desirous*) ; or a substantive preceded by هم (hem); as, هم اشانه
(hem-ashyane), *of the same nest ;* هَمْجِنْس (hem-jıns), *of the same
genus ;* همشهری (hem-shehrı), *of the same town or country, a
fellow-countryman ;* of a substantive followed by وش (vesh),
like ; as, پریوش (perı-vesh), *fairy-like ;* of a substantive
followed by رنگ (rang), فام (fam), or گُون (gyun), all signifying
colour ; as, سَبز (sebz-rang), *green-coloured ;* زمرد (zumurråd-
fam), *emerald-coloured ;* گندم گُون (gendum-gyun), *wheat-coloured*
(i. e., *dark-complexioned, brown*) ; of a substantive followed by
کار (kyar, gyar), گَر (ger), بان (ban), or دَار (dar) ; as, شیرین کار
(shırın-kyar), *sweet-mannered ;* افرید گار (aferıd-gyar), *creative*

(i. e., *creator*) ; زَرگَر (zer-ger), *goldworker, goldsmith* ; بَاغبَان
(bag-ban), *garden-keeper* (i. e., *gardener*) ; مُهردَار (muhr-dar), *seal-
keeper* ; or followed by دَان (dan), زَار (zar), سَار (sar), or اِستَان
(istan), all names of special places ; as, قَلمدَان (qalem-dan), *a
pen-case* ; كُلزَار (gyúl-zar), *a flower-garden, a flowery mead* ;
كوهسَار (kyuh-sar), *mountainous district* ; عربِستَان ('arabistan),
Arabia ; or a substantive repeated ; as, حَاكحَاك (chak-chak),
imitative of the sound of repeated blows with axe or sword ;
the same, or two different substantives, with ا placed between
them ; as, حَاكيَاحَاك (chakya-chak), same signification, سراپَا (ser-
a-pa), *from head to foot* ; or with تَا or ت in place of the ا ; as,
سَرتَاپَا (ser-ta-pa), same sense ; سَرتَسَر (ser-te-ser), *from end to end,
from beginning to end* ; or with ان ا in شَانروز (sheban-ruz), *night
and day* (which is unique), شَانهروز (shebane-ruz), meaning :
*a whole night and day, all night and all day, twenty-four hours,
or several nights and days in one succession* ; or with some
other Persian preposition between the two ; as, سدرپی pey-der-
pey), *step by step, gradatim* ; دستبردست (dest-ber-dest), *hand
on hand, hands crossed* ; سِنهبسِنه (sine-be-sine), *breast to breast* ;
دُوشَادُوش (dush-a-dush), *shoulder to shoulder, back to back* ; سَربمُهر
(ser-be-muhr), *with the head* (or mouth of a bag, bottle, &c.)
sealed up ; or with a substantive and compound adjective ; as,
بَخت برگَشتَه (bakht-ber-geshte), *whose luck is reversed* ; or even

four words combined; as, سربفلك كشیده (ser-be-felek-keshīde), *whose head is lifted up to the very spheres*; besides many other varieties; especially the two privatives in بی (bī), *without*, and نا (na), *not*; as, بی ادب (bī-edeb), *without education or manners, unmannerly, impolite*; نابینا (na-bīna), *not seeing, sightless, blind.*

Some Arabic expressions may be regarded as compound epithets in Turkish and Persian; as, صاحبقران (sahib-qīran), *lord of the conjunction* (i. e., *the master of the age*); ولی نعمت (veli-ni'met), *associate of benefits* (i. e., *a benefactor*); expressions formed of ذو (zu), ذات (zat), اهل (ehl), and ارباب (erbab), all of which imply *possession*; as, ذو ذوابه (zu-zuabe), *possessed of a forelock or topknot*, and ذو ذنابه (zu-zunabe), *possessed of a following* (i.e., *a comet*); ذات الجنب (zatu-'l-jenb, *vulg.* satlıjan), *the possessor of the side* (i. e., *pleurisy*); or in Persian construction; as, اهل عرض (ehli-'irz), *possessed of honour or virtue, honorable, honest, virtuous*; ارباب مسند (erbabı-mesned), *those who possess the chief seat* (i. e., *high dignitaries*); or an adjective qualified with غیر (ġáyr), *other*; as, غیر محدود (ġayrı-mahdud), *other than circumscribed* (i. e., *unlimited, undefined*); or an Arabic verb in the aorist made negative with لا (la), *not*; as, لایحصی (la-yuhsa), *not to be counted, innumerable*; لایعد (la-yu'add), *untold, innumerable*; لایموت (la-yemut), *who dies not, immortal*; لایتجزا (la-yetejezza), *not to be subdivided, indivisible*; or an

Ar.bic adjective followed by a definite article and substantive; as, اَبَدِىُّ ٱلدَّوَامِ (ebediyyu-'d-devam), *eternal in duration*; قَوِىُّ الْبُنْيَانِ (qaviyyu-'l-bunyan), *strong in build*; &c., &c., &c.

Every Turkish adjective is also an adverb; that is to say, that, without any modification of form, the Turkish adjective qualifies verbs as well as substantives; thus, كُوزَلْ آتْ (gyuzel at), *a beautiful stallion*; كُوزَلْ يُورُمَكْ (gyuzel yurumek), *to walk gracefully*. The same is the case with Persian adjectives, whether used in Turkish or in Persian phrases. Arabic adjectives, as Arabic substantives, require to be put in their own accusative case indefinite when used as adverbs; as, فِعْلًا (fi'lau), *by act*; حَسَنًا (hasanan), *beautifully*. Arabic substantives are also sometimes used as Turkish adverbs by being put in their own genitive, indefinite or definite, as may be, and preceded by an Arabic preposition; as, عَنْ غَفْلَة ('an gafletin), *by inadvertence*; عَلَى التَّوَالِى ('ale-'t-tevali), *in continued succession, successively*; فِى الْحَقِيقَة (fi-'l-haqiqa), *in reality, really, truly*; بِالدَّفَعَات (bi-'d-defa'at), *on several occasions, repeatedly*; لِسَبَبٍ (li-sebebin), *for a reason*; &c.

As with substantives, so also every Turkish adjective has its diminutive, formed by the addition of the suffix جـه (je, ja), *-ish*, to the word, whether this end in a consonant or vowel; as, يَشِل (yeshil), *green*, يَشِلْجَه (yeshilje), *greenish, somewhat green*; قِزِل (qizil) *red*, قِزِلْجَه (qiziljá) *reddish*; بُويُوك (biyuk)

large, بیوكجه (bìyukje) *largish;* اوفاق (ùfaq) *small,* اوفاقجه
(ufaqja) *smallish;* ابرى (ìrì) *large,* ابریجه (ìrìjè) *largish;* قره
(qara) *black,* قرهجه (qaràja) *blackish;* قورو (qùrù) *dry,* قوروجه
(qùruja) *dryish.* A modification of this form, dictated by the
principle of euphony, is used for the words اوفاق, كچولك, سوك,
by substituting a final ك or ق for the ه, and suppressing those
letters at the end of the radical word, as for substantives; thus,
بیوجك (bìyujek), *largish.* A further conformity with the sense
of euphony, avoiding two اوستون vowels in succession, makes
اوفاجق (ufajìq) *smallish,* and كوجك (kuchujuk) *smallish;* this
last being doubly euphonic.

These diminutive adjectives, as in every language, often
express in Turkish the reverse of diminution in the quality
they represent, being in fact exaggeratives in sense, and meaning *very, exceedingly, extremely,* &c.; as, حسورجه آدم در (jesurja
adam dìr), *he is a bravish man* (i. e., *a very brave man*).

Section III. *The Numerals.*

Turkish, Arabic, and Persian numerals, cardinal and ordinal,
are used in Ottoman. Arabic fractions are also used as far as
one-tenth. In this sketch, however, the five sorts of Turkish
numerals alone are explained. These are the cardinal, ordinal,
distributive, fractional, and indefinite numbers.

The simple Turkish cardinal numbers are : بِرْ (bĭr) *one*,
ایكی (ĭkĭ) *two*, اُوُچْ (uch) *three*, درت (durt) *four*, بَشْ (besh) *five*,
اَلْتی (altĭ) *six*, یَدی (yedĭ) *seven*, سَكِزْ (sekĭz) *eight*, طُقُوزْ (doqŭz)
nine, اُونْ (ŏn) *ten*, یِگْرِمی (yĭyĭrmĭ) *twenty*, اوبوزْ (otŭz), *thirty*,
قِرْقْ (qĭrq) *forty*, اللِی (ellĭ) *fifty*, اَلْتمِشْ (altmĭsh) *sixty*, یَتمِشْ (yet-
mĭsh) *seventy*, سَكسَانْ (seksan) *eighty*, طُقسَانْ (dŏqsan) *ninety*,
یُوزْ (yŭz) *a hundred*, بِكْ (bĭn) *a thousand*. The two substantives, یُكْ (yŭk), *a hundred thousand*, and مِلْیُونْ (mĭlyŏn), *a
million*, are also used ; but they are not true numerals. They
are names of aggregates, and require the numerals before
them ; as, بِرْ یُكْ (bĭr yŭk), *one hundred thousand*, بِرْ مِلْیُونْ (bĭr
mĭlyon) *one million* ; and so on for higher numbers, ایكِی یُكْ,
اون ملیون, &c. The French numerals بلیُونْ (bĭlyŏn), تِرِلْیُونْ (tĭrĭl-
yŏn), &c., are sometimes used.

The compound Turkish cardinal numerals are uniformly
built up by putting the units after the tens up to 99, and by
placing the word یُوزْ before the simple or compound expression
up to 199 ; then by adding the units from 2 to 9 before یوز
up to 999 ; next by using بِكْ before these simples or compounds up to 1999 ; and finally, by again using the simples
or compounds before بِكْ up to 999,999 ; thus, اُونْبِرْ (ŏn-bĭr)
eleven, یِگْرمی ایكی (yĭyĭrmĭ ĭkĭ) *twenty-two*, یوز اوبوز اوچ (yuz ŏtŭz
ûch) *one hundred and thirty-three*, بِكْ سَكِزْیُوزْ قِرْقْ بَشْ (bĭn

sekiz yuz qîrq besh) *one thousand eight hundred and forty-five,*

بش يوُزْاَلْتمِشْ سَكِزْ بيكْ يوُزْ اوُندِرْت (bèsh yûz âltmîsh sèkîz bîñ yûz

ôn durt) 568,114, اوُچ مِليوُنْ يدى يوُكْ طُقْسَانْ اِيكى بِكْ اوُجيُوز الـلى آلْتى

(uch mîlyon, yedî yuk, dôqsân îkî bîn, ûch yûz, èllî âltî)

3,792,356. It will be noticed that no conjunction enters these

combinations. When the foreign expression ١٠٠ وِن, or the

treasury word يوُك is not used, the native method of expressing

multiples of يوُزْبِاشْ is to state the simple or compound

number of such multiple, and then to intercalate the word

كَرَّه (kerre) *times,* before the word يوُزْبِكْ; as, يدى كَرَّه يوُزْبِكْ

(yedî kerrè yûz bîn) *seven times one hundred thousand,* 700,000;

درت يوُز الـلى اِيكى كَرَّه يوُزْبِكْ (durt yuz ellî îkî kerrè yuz bîn)

45,200,000.

The Turkish interrogative cardinal numeral is قَاچْ (qach)

how many ?

The cardinal numerals are adjectives; but, like all adjec-

tives, may be used as substantives, and declined. Even the

interrogative قَاچْ is used as a substantive when enquiring

"*what number ?*" or "*what is it o'clock ?*" or "*at what price ?*"

or "*what is the day of the month ?*" Thus : قَاچْ دِيدِنِكْز (qach

dîdînîz) "*how many did you say ?*" سَاعَتْ قَاچَه كَلْدى (sâ'ât qâchâ

galdî) "*to how many (hours) has the clock come ?*" قَاچَه ويرِيوُرْسِينْ

(qâchâ verîyôrsun) "*at how much art thou selling (it, them) ?*"

اَلك فاچی دُر (ayĭñ qachĭ dĭr) "*the how-manyeth of the month is it?*"

The Persian compound cardinals place the higher elements first, as in Turkish and English; but the conjunction و is introduced between each two members; as, هزار و دُوِیست و شصت و هفت (hezar ú duwĭst u shast u heft), *a thousand, two hundred, and sixty-seven.*

The Arabic compound cardinals take the conjunction و between each pair also; but the lower elements stand first; as, سَنَه تسْعُ وخَمْسِین و ماَتَن وَاَلْف (sene-i tĭs' ú khamsin ú mŀeteyn u elf) *the year one thousand two hundred and fifty-nine,* expressed in Turkish, دك اـكـیـُوز اَلْلِی طُقُوزْ سَنَه (bĭn ĭkĭyuz ellĭ dŏqŭz sénesĭ).

The Turkish ordinal numbers are formed by adding an esere to the last quiescent consonant of the cardinal, simple or compound, followed by the termination نُجِی; as, بِرِنْجِی (bĭrĭnjĭ) *first,* اوزوزِجِ (otŭzunju) *thirtieth,* یوزنْجِی (yuzunjŭ) *hundredth,* بِیكِنْجِی (bĭnĭnjĭ) *thousandth,* اَللِی سَكِزِنْجِی بِیك بَشْیُوز فرق طُقُوزنْجِی. But, in the numbers that end in vowel ی, this is suppressed before the same termination; as, یِلنْجِی (ĭkĭnjĭ) *second,* التِنْجِی (altĭnjĭ) *sixth,* یدِجِی (yedĭnjĭ) *seventh,* سـكـرمنْجِی (yĭyĭrmĭnjĭ) *twentieth,* اللِنْجِی (ellĭnjĭ) *fiftieth.* The cardinal دُرْت changes its final into د before the ordinal termination; as, اُون دردنْجِی (ŏn-dŭrdunju) *fourteenth.*

The Arabic and Persian ordinals are frequently used, and may be found in the lexicons, &c.

The Turkish distributive numbers are formed from the cardinals by making their last quiescent consonant movent with û̆stun, and then adding a quiescent ٰ to the word ; as, بَرّ (bírèr), بَشَرْ (bèshèr), أُوتُوزَرْ (ŏtùzèr); يُوزَرْ (yùzèr), بِيكَرْ (bíñèr). Their sense is expressed in English, which has no such numerals, by the words *each* and *apiece* ; the foregoing examples will thus be rendered : *one each, five apiece, thirty each, a hundred each, a thousand each.* The cardinal دَرْت becomes دَرْدَرْ (dùrder) *four apiece.*

When the cardinal ends with a vowel, the syllable شَر (sher) is suffixed to form the distributive ; as, اِكِشَرْ (íkísher) *two apiece,* اَلتِيشَرْ (àltísher) *six each,* يَدِيشَرْ (yedísher) *seven apiece,* يِكِرْمِشَرْ (yíyírmísher) *twenty each,* اللِّشَرْ (ellísher) *fifty each.*

In the case of more than one hundred or thousand, it is the cardinal that designates their number that receives the distributive suffix ; as, اِكِشَرْ يُوز (íkísher yuz) *two hundred each,* بَشَر بِيْن (besher bín) *five thousand apiece.* And in compound numbers the distributive suffixes are added to the numbers of thousands, of hundreds, and of final units or tens, to indicate one distribution ; thus, بَشَرْ يُوزْ يِكِرْمِى بِرَرْ (besher yùz yíyírml bírer) *five hundred and twenty-one each,* سَكِزَرْ بِيْك يَدِيشَرْ يُوزقِرقِ اِكِشَرْ (seklzer bln, yedísher yuz, qîrq íkísher), 8,742 *apiece ;* يُوْ اللِّشَرْ (yùz ellísher), 150 *each.*

The Turkish fractional numbers are very simple. The number of the denominator in the locative, and followed by the number of the numerator is the form; as, ايكيده بر (ikide bir) *in two* (parts), *one; i.e.* ½, *the half;* نشده ايكى (beshde iki) *in five, two;* *i.e.* ⅖, *two-fifths.* Sometimes one of the synonyms پاى (pay), حزّ (juz'), قسم (qism), حصّه (hissa) *part*, is added after each numeral of the fraction; as, ايك ناوده بر پاى (iki payda, bir pay) *in two parts, one part.*

The Arabic fractional numbers are also used up to ten. Excepting the word نصف (nisf) *a half, the half*, they are all of the form فعل; thus, ثلث (suls, *vulg.* sulus) *a third*, ربع (rub') *a fourth*, خمس (khums) *a fifth*, سدس (suds) *a sixth*, سبع (sub') *a seventh*, ثمن (sumn) *an eighth*, تسع (tus') *a ninth*, عشر ('ushr, *vulg.* 'ushur) *a tenth, a tithe.* The dual of ثلث is used, ثلثان (sulsan) *two-thirds;* but for all the others a Turkish numerator is used; as, اوچ ربع (uch rub') *three quarters*, ايكى خمس (iki khums) *two-fifths*, بش تسع (besh tus') *five-ninths*, &c.

There are two special Turkish adjectives and one Turkish substantive to express *half.* One of the adjectives, يارم (yarim), and the substantive, يارى (yari), signify *the half* (of one sole thing; as, يارم الما (yarim elma) *half an apple, a half apple;* ألمانك ياريسى (elmanin yarisi), *the half of an* (or *of the*) *apple.* The other adjective, بوچوق (buchuq), is used after some whole number, never alone ; as, بر بوچوق اَلمَا (bĭr buchuq elma) *an apple and a half,* ايكى بوچوق ساعت (ĭkĭ búchuq sa'at) *two hours and a half.*

When a complex fractional number consisting of an integer and a fraction other than *one-half* has to be expressed, the Turkish or Arabic fractions are used, the conjunction و or the preposition ٱله being introduced between the integer and the fraction; as, ايكى ايله بر ربع or ايكى و بر ربع *two and one-fourth.* When the Turkish fraction is used, the numeral بِر in the genitive is also introduced before the fraction ; as, بش ايله براك سَكِزْدَه أوچى *five, and three-eighths of one.*

The indefinite numerals are : هَر (her) *every ;* هَر بِر (her bĭr) *every one, each ;* هِيچ (hĭch) *no, none ;* هِيچ بِر (hĭch bĭr), *no ;* بَعْض (ba'zĭ) *some ;* اَكْثَر (ekser) *the most part ;* بِرْقَاچ (bĭr qach) *some, a few ;* آز (az) *few ;* چوق (choq) *many ;* بِر آز (bĭr az) *a few, a little ;* برچوق (bĭr chóq) *a great many, a great quantity ;* &c. Of these, هَر is always an adjective; the rest are adjectives and substantives.

There is a small series of Turkish numerals of a peculiar nature, from ابكِز (ĭkĭz), *twin, twins,* through اوچيز (uchuz) *triple, a trine,* دردِز (dúrdúz) *fourfold,* to بَشِز (beshĭz) *five-fold,* and perhaps on to اونِز (ónúz) *ten-fold.* Adjectives are formed

from these in لو ; as, ايكزلو (ikizlı̇), *possessed of twins, of twin*
(branches, &c.) ; اوچيزلو (ůchuzlu) *with three* (lambs, branches,
&c.) ; &c.

The written digits are : ١ 1, ٢ 2, ٣ 3, ٤ 4, ٥ 5, ٦ 6, ٧ 7, ٨ 8,
٩ 9, . 0. With these, compound numbers are written as in
English, from left to right ; as, ٢٥ 25, ١٦٠ 160, ٣٤٠٩ 3409,
٧٨٠٠٣٠٤٦ 78003046, &c.

In dates, the thousand, and generally the hundreds. of the
year of the Hijra are omitted, as also the dots of the letters ;
thus, ١ــــه stands for ١ــــه (sene bı̇n ı̇kı̇yuz dóqsan altı̇)
in the year (of the Hijra) 1296 ; فى ٢١ دا سه (fı̇ yı̇yı̇rmı̇ bı̇r
za, sene 97) *on the 21st Zı̇-'l-Qada, '97* (A.H.).

The signs for the months, in dates, are : ه, for مُحَرَّم ; ص, for
; جماذى ٱلأَوَّل, for حا ; رَبِيعُ ٱلآخِرْ for ر, ; رَبِيعُ ٱلأَوَّل for رل, ; صفر را,
; رمضان for ـر, ; حماذى الاخر for ـس, ; شعبان for ـس, ; رجب for ـس, ; شعبان for ـں, for ـب ;
ل, for شَوَّالْ ; دا, for ذى ٱلْـقَـعْـدَه ; د, for ذى لْحَجّه. The day
always precedes the sign of the month ; and the first day is
termed عره (gurre), while the thirtieth is named سَلَ (selkh) ;
as, سه ه عره فى سه ص سا فى ; all dots being omitted in
these shortened numeral dates. Not so, however, when the
date is written out in full words ; as, اشــمـو يـلى انكو طُـقْسَان (ı̇shbu bı̇n
ı̇kı̇yuz dóqsan dóqůz sene'l hı̇jrı̇yyesı̇ mah-ı̇ muharremı̇nı̇n ón

beshlnjl penjshenblh gyůnů) *This day of Thursday, the 15th of
the month of Muharrem, of the Hijra year* 1299.

Section IV. *The Pronoun.*

The Turkish personal pronoun has no distinction of gender:
بن (ben) *I,* سن (san, *not* sen) *thou,* اول (ŏ; in writing, generally,
اول ŏl) *he, she, it ;* and their plurals : بز (blz) *we,* سز (slz) *you,*
اَنْلَر (anlar, onlar) *they.*

In politeness, بز and سـز are used instead of بن and سـن.
They then have their own plurals: بزلر (blzler), سزلر (slzler),
which cannot be expressed in English. These are even used
as singulars, by the over-polite. The third person plural is
used, in the same way, out of politeness, for the singular, as
is practised in Italian ; but it has not its plural. The word
كندی (kendl) *self,* is a kind of common pronoun, of all the
persons, singular and plural. It is specialized by the possessives.

The personal pronouns, singular and plural, are declined in
the same way as the nouns substantive, excepting that some of
them have a special genitive,—all but those of the second
person, singular and plural. These genitives are : بنم (benlm)
of me, my ; سنك (sanln) *of thee, thy ;* انك (anln, ŏnuñ) *of him,
her, it ; his, her, its ;* بزم (blzlm) *of us, our;* سزك (slzln) *of you,
your ;* انلرك (anlarln, onlarln) *of them, their.* But, to take either

of the prepositions ایچون , الہ , after their singulars, they must
be put in the genitive, all but the third person plural; as,

بنم ایچون *for me,* سزك الہ *with you,* انك ایچون *for him, her, it,* انلر ایہ
with them.

These genitives are used, *when required,* to emphasize and
corroborate the possessive pronoun of the same number and
person. They are never used alone, without their possessives
to corroborate; thus, بابام (babam) my *father* (*not* my *mother,*
&c.), بنم بابام (benim babam) *my* father (not *your* father, or *his*
father).

The possessive pronouns, too, have no distinction of gender,
either on the English or French principle. They are ؞ (im,
îm) *my;* ك (in, în) *thy;* ی (i, î), or, after a vowel, سی (si, sî)
his, her, its; مز (imiz, îmîz) *our,* كز (iniz, înîz) *your;* لری (leri,
larî), *their.*

These possessives are suffixed to the substantives they
qualify, and form one word with them. That compound
word is then declined like a simple substantive; thus, اویم
(evim) *my house,* اویمك (evimin) *of my house,* اویمه (evime) *to
my house,* اویمده (evimde) *in my house;* &c. (The ی added
here before the bare possessive, is thought by some to be
needed in the case of a preceding consonant that does not
join on in writing to its next letter in the same word. Others
do not consider it necessary, and write: اویم , اوك , اوی , &c.; but

when the compound, in declension, &c., takes another vowel
after it, it is more usual to add this preceding vowel also; as,
اوِكزْ (evlmln) *of my house,* اوِمَه (evlme) *to my house;* اوِمَك
(evlnlz) *your house;* &c.

The vowel that precedes the bare possessive is an esere, soft
or hard, given grammatically to the final consonant of the
qualified substantive, when it ends in a consonant. Thus,
ات (åt) *a horse,* اتم (atîm) *my horse,* اتكْ (atîn) *thy horse,* اتی
(atî), *his, her, its horse,* اتمز (atîmîz) *our horse,* اتكز (atînîz)
your horse, اتلری (atlarî) *their horse.* After an uturu vowel
dominant, this eserè becomes uturu also; thus, اوغل (òghùl)
a son, اوغلم (oghùlum) *my son;* بوت (but) *a thigh,* بوتم (butùm)
or بودم (budùm) *my thigh;* يوز (yuz) *a face,* يوزم (yuzum) *my
face;* كوز (gyùz) *an eye,* كوزم (gyuzum) *my eye.*

When the substantive ends with a vowel, the bare possessive
is added to form a syllable with that vowel, whatever it may
be; thus, بابام (babam) *my father;* يانقوك (yanqon) *thy echo;*
قوسی (qapusu) *his, her, its door* or *gate;* سونكومز (sungyumuz)
our bayonet; كوركوكز (gyurgyuùuz) *your experience;* سورولری
(surulerî) *their flock.* The example here given, with the
possessive singular of the third person, shows clearly that
when the substantive ends with a vowel, سی is the possessive,
in lieu of ی after a consonant.

If the final vowel of the substantive is ه, it is never joined on to the possessive in writing. Thus, تَـيِّـزهم (teyzem) *my* (maternal) *aunt*, تيزهك (teyzen), *thy aunt*, ﺗﺰهسی (teyzesi) *his* or *her aunt*; تَـزهمز (teyzemiz) *our aunt*, تيزهكز (teyzeniz) *your aunt*, ﺗﺰهلری (teyzeleri) *their aunt*.

When the final vowel is ی, the possessives of the first and second persons singular do not join on to it in writing. In the third person singular, and in all the possessive plurals, they join on. Thus, تَرزی (terzi) *a tailor*, تَـرزیم (terzim) *my tailor*, ترزیك (terzin) *thy tailor*, ترزیسی (terzisi) *his* or *her tailor*, ترزیمز (terzimiz) *our tailor*, ترزیکز (terziniz) *your tailor*, ترزیلری (terzileri) *their tailor*. There is no valid reason for this rule; custom alone has it so. Thus are formed: كـندم (kendim) *myself*, كندك (kendin) *thyself*, كندسی (kendisi) *his, her, itself*; كندمز (kendimiz) *ourselves*, كندكز (kendiniz) *yourselves*, كندلری (kéndiléri) *theirselves*.

A final ق, in a polysyllable, as in declension, changes into غ before the possessives, singular or plural, excepting that of the third person plural; so also, an Arabic ك changes into Turkish ك (*y* value) in like cases. Thus, قوناق (qonaq), *a mansion*, قوناعم (qonaghim) *my mansion*; اپك (ipek) *silk*, اپكك (ipeyin) *thy silk*; طاوق (tawuq) *a fowl*, طاوغی (tawughu) *his* or *her fowl*; قوناعمز (qonaghimiz) *our mansion*, اپیكز (ipeyiniz) *your silk*; طاوقلری (tawuqlari) *their fowl*. The

reason of the exception is evident,—the final consonant takes
no vowel before لَرِى.

These possessives equally qualify plural substantives, and
follow the sign of the plural. Thus, اَوْلَرِم (evlerĭm), *my houses;*
اَتْلَرِڭ (ătlărĭn) *thy horses;* سُوڭْكُولَرِى (sŭngyulerĭ) *his, her, its
bayonets;* سُورُولَرِمِز (sŭrŭlerĭmĭz) *our flocks;* تَيْزَهْ لَرِڭِز (teyzelerĭ-
ĭnĭz) *your aunts;* قُوناقلَرِى (qonaqlarĭ) *their mansions.*

By a consideration of the examples above given with the
possessives of the third persons, singular and plural, as
attached to singular and plural substantives, two peculiarities
become evident, namely: 1, the plural sign is not repeated for
the possessive when the substantive is itself plural; 2, consequently, the combination of a substantive and a possessive
of the third person, when it has the plural syllable لَرْ between
the two, leaves it altogether doubtful whether this plural sign
belongs to the substantive or to the possessive. Even if the
combination قُوناقْلَرْلَرِى (qonaqlarlerĭ) had been in use,—which
is not the case,—it would have been impossible to decide
whether قُوناقلَرِى (qonaqlarĭ) was intended to betoken the sense
of *his* or *her mansions,* on the one hand, or *their mansion,* on
the other. Add to this difficulty the third sense of *their mansions,* and the puzzle becomes still more complicated. In
conversation, the doubt of the hearer may be removed, if
necessary, by proper enquiries. But, in a written document,

intended to be understood by an absent reader, possibly after the death of the writer, a method was seen, especially by judges and legists, to be necessary for distinguishing between the three cases.

That distinction is effected, in writing, somewhat at the expense of plain grammar, as follows. To distinguish the single possessor of the plural possessions, the singular corroborative genitive of the personal pronoun is placed before the combination containing the plural sign; thus, اَنْك مُونَاقْلَرِى (anîn qónaqlarî) *his* or *her mansions*. To distinguish the plural joint possessors of a single possession, the genitive of the plural personal pronoun is prefixed, and grammar is violated by omitting the plural sign from the combination of substantive and possessive; as, انلارِك قوزْ'غى (anlarîn qonaghî) *their mansion*. In the third case, the sign of the plural is used in the corroborative and in the combination; thus, انلارِك مونَاقلَرِى (anlarîn qónaqlarî) *their mansions*. A doubt may still be felt, and these distinctions are not always used.

The declension of the combination with the possessive of the third person, singular or plural, takes a special form, a ن being introduced before the prepositions, and the final vowel-letter of the original combination suppressed before this ن, when the latter is joined in writing to the combination singular, or does not itself possess a vowel in the combination plural. This rule, applied to possessives joined to substantives ending respectively in consonants or vowels, acts thus:

كِتَابْلَرِينْكْ ; كِتَابِنْدَنْ , كِتَابِنْدَه , كِتَابِنَه , كِتَابِنِى , كِتَابِكْ , كِتَابِى ,

تَيْزَهسِنَه , تَيْزَهسِنْكْ , تَيْزَهسِى ; كِتَابْلَرِنْدَنْ , كِتَابْلَرِينِى , كِتَابْلَرِنْدَه , كِتَابْلَرِينَه ,

تَيْزَهلَرِنْدَه , تَيْزَهلَرِينَه , تَيْزَهلَرِينْكْ , تَيْزَهلَرِى , تَيْزَهسِنْدَنْ ; تَيْزَهسِنِى , تَيْزَهسِنْدَه ,

تَيْزَهلَرِنْدَنْ , تَيْزَهلَرِينِى .

When كَنْدِى is an adjective, it remains unchanged, and means *own*; thus, كَنْدِى بَابَام (kendí bâbâm) *my own father*, كَنْدِى وَالِدَهلَرِيكِزْ (kendí vālîdelerînîz) *your own mothers*, &c.

SECTION V. *The Demonstratives.*

These are, بُو (bû) *this*, شُو (shû) *that* or *this*, أُو (ô) or أُول (ôl, as in the personal) *that*, أُوبِرْ (ô-bîr) or أُولْبِرْ (ol-bîr) *the other*. They are used as substantives and as adjectives; being declined or invariable, accordingly, like other substantives and adjectives. Thus, بُو كِتَاب *this book*, بُو كِتَابْلَرْ *these books*; أُوبِرْ آدَمْ *that other man*, أُوبِرْ آدَمْلَرْ *those other men*; &c.

As substantives, بُو and شُو are thus declined, something like the personal أُو or أُول : بُو (bû), بُونُكْ (bûnûn), بُوكَا (bûna), بُونْدَه (bunda), بُونْلَرِكْ (bûnlarîn), بُونْلَرَه (bûnlârâ), بُونْلَرْدَه (bûnlârdâ), بُونْرَى (bûnlarî),

بُونْزَ (bûnlardan) ; شُو (shû, sometimes written شُول, pronounced shôl), شُونُكْ (shûnûñ), شُوكَ (shûna), شونده (shûnda),
شُونُ (shûnû), شوندن (shûndan) ; شونلر (shûnlar), شُونْلَرِكْ (shûn-
larîn), شُونْلَرَه (shûnlâra) ; شُونْلَرْدَه (shûnlarda), شونلرى (shûnlarî),
شُونْلَرْدَنْ (shûnlârdân). With اِيجُونْ and اللَه their singulars are
put in the genitive ; as, بُونُكْ اِيجُونْ *for this,* شُونُكْ اللَه *with that.*

But أُورْ , to be used as a substantive, must have the possessive suffix of the third person appended to it ; اوبرى (o-bîrî)
its other one, the other one (of the two). It is then declined
like all similar combinations : أُوبِرِينِكْ , أُوبِرِينَه , أُوبِرِينْدَه , أُوبِرِينِى,
أُوبِرْلَرِنْدَنْ . أُوبِرْلَرِينِى , أُوبِرْلَرِنْدَه , أُوبِرْلَرِينَه , أُوبِرْلَرِينْكْ , أُوبِرْلَرِى ; أُوبِرِنْدَنْ
Or it may take either of the two possessive suffixes of the first
and second persons plural ; as, أُوبِرِيمِزْ (ô-bîrîmîz), *the other one*
of us, أُوبِرِيمِزكْ *of the other one of us ;* أُوبِرِيمْزَه *to the other one of*
you ; اوبرلريمزده *in the other ones of us ·* اوبرلريكزى *the other ones*
of you ; &c.

SECTION VI. *The Interrogatives.*

كِيمْ (kîm) *who?* is always a substantive, and declined as
such, singular and plural: كِيمُكْ *of whom? whose?* كِيمَه *to whom ?*
كِيمْدَه *in whom ?* كِيمِى *whom ?* كِيمْدَنْ *of* or *from whom ?* كِيمْلَرْ
who, what or *which persons ?* &c.

نه (ne) *what?* is generally a substantive, and declined; but it is also used as an adjective, and is then invariable: نه‌ك (nenīn) *of what?* نه‌یه (for نه‌یه, neye) *to what?* نه‌ده (nede) *in what?* نه‌یی (neyī) *what* (accus.)? نه‌دن (for نه‌دن, nedan) *from what?* نه‌لر (for نه‌لر, neler) *what* (things)? نه‌لرك (nelerīn) *of what* (things); &c.

قنغی (qangī, *vulg.* hangī) *which?* is both substantive and adjective,—declined or invariable accordingly.

These three words, as substantives, take the possessive suffixes. Thus, كیمیم (kīmīm) *my who?* نه‌م (nem) *my what?* كیمك (kīmīñ) *thy who?* نه‌ك (nen) *thy what?* قنغی‌سی (qāngī-sī) *its which, which* (one) *of it?* كیملریم (kīmlerīm) *my what persons?* نه‌لریم (nelerīm) *my what things?* قنغیمز (qangīmīz) *which* (one) *of us?* قنغیلریكز (qangīlerīnīz) *which* (ones) *of you?* قنغیلری (qangīlerī) *which* (one, or, which ones) *of them?*

نه قدر (for نه قدر) or نقدر (*vulg.* nāqadar) *how much?* نه درلی (*vulg.* ne turlu) *what sort?* ⎱ are both substantives and ⎰ adjectives.

Section VII. *The Relative Pronoun.*

THERE IS NO RELATIVE PRONOUN IN TURKISH, though attempts are made to use the Persian relative and conjunction, که (kī), as such, in literary composition. The Turkish *conjunction* که is a very different thing. Its use by Europeans

peans and others, as a relative pronoun, is greatly to be
avoided. This avoidance of all use of the relative pronoun
is the prime distinction of Turkish from all Aryan and Semitic
tongues. It is the perfection of language.

The numerous active and passive participles of the Turkish
verb obviate the necessity of a relative. The active participles take the place of our relative when it is nominative
to a verb ; and the passive participles do so when our relative
is the accusative, or any indirect object of a verb. (See this
explained in the paragraphs on the Participles, in Section VIII.,
on the Verb.)

There is a peculiar Turkish relative, however, to which we
have no parallel in English,—the suffix ﻚﯽ (kĭ). It is attached
to nouns and pronouns substantive in two ways. If the substantive be in the genitive, the combination is a substantive,
and indicates *that which belongs to* (the substantive) ; thus,
بابا, بابانك, بابانڭكﯽ (babanĭnkĭ) *the one which belongs to a* (or
the) *father*, بابامڭكﯽ (babamĭñkĭ) *the one which belongs to my
father*, باباسﻨﯔكﯽ (babásĭnĭnkĭ) *the one belonging to his* (or *her*)
father, his father's one ; &c. If the substantive be in the
locative case, the combination is sometimes a substantive,
sometimes an adjective. The substantive combination then
indicates *that which exists in* (the simple substantive) ; the
adjective combination expresses *the* (substantive) *which exists*

in (the first substantive). Thus, بابمدکی (babamdekı) *the thing, the one that exists, that is in* (the possession or keeping of) *my father, which my father has or holds;* باباسندکی علم (babasîndekî 'ilim) *the science possessed by his father, that is in his father.* The substantive combinations form the plural, and are declined; the adjective combination is invariable.

With a noun of place or of time the same particle, کی, forms a relative combination, substantive or adjective, having relation to the place or time named. In the case of the noun of place, the locative preposition may also be employed. Thus, اشاع *the foot,* or *lower part,* اشاعت and اشاعیده *that which is at the foot;* خشم *the evening,* اخشامی *that which was or will be* (present) *in the evening.*

SECTION VIII. *The Derivation of the Verb.*

As a general rule, each primary Turkish verb forms, itself included, a system of twelve *affirmative,* twelve *negative,* and twelve *impotential* verbs, by regular derivation ;—thirty-six in all ; one half being verbs *active,* the other half verbs *passive;* the active verbs being *transitive* or *intransitive;* the passives having for their nominative the direct or the indirect object of the transitive, the indirect object only of the intransitive primitive.

In another mode of subdivision, on the other hand, these

thirty-six verbs divide into two equal classes, in pairs, one of each pair being *simple*, and the other *causative* (which is also *permissive*, as the sense may show).

Each simple and causative pair of verbs is either *determinate*, *indeterminate*, or *reciprocal;* so that, by a special division of the same thirty-six, there are twelve determinate, twelve indeterminate, and twelve reciprocal verbs; thus (giving the imperatives of each, for economy of space):—

ACTIVE.

CLASSES.	TRANS. OR INTRANS. Determinate.	TRANS. OR INTRANS. Indeterminate.	INTRANSITIVE. Reciprocal.
AFFIRMATIVE Simple	تپ (tĕp) kick (him); kick.	تپن (tĕpln) kick about, dance (in pain, with joy, &c.).	تپلش (tĕplsh) kick mutually one another.
AFFIRMATIVE Causative (Permissive)	تپدر (tĕpdlr) make or let (him) be kicked; ...kick.	تپدر (tĕpludlr) make (him) kick about.	تپشدر (tĕplsŋdlr) make (they kic.; mutually one nother.
NEGATIVE Simple	تپم (tĕpm') kick (him) not ; k k not.	تپن (tĕp n ä) kick not about.	تپشم (t p'shmä) kick no m tua' y one ano her.
NEGATIVE Causative (Permissive)	تپدرم (tĕpdlrmä) make or let not (hi n) be kicked; ...kick.	تپندرم (tĕplndlrmä) make not (him) kick about.	تپشدرم (tĕplshdlrmä) make (them) not kick one another mutually.
IMPOTENTIAL Simple	تپمم (tĕpдmĕ) be unable to ick (him); ... to kick.	تپنمم (tĕplnĕmĕ) be unable to kick about.	تپشمم (tĕplshĕmĕ) be unable to kick one another mutually.
IMPOTENTIAL Causative (Permissive)	تپدرمم (tĕpdlrêmĕ) be unable to make (him) be kicked: ..kick.	تپندرمم (tĕplndlrêmĕ) be unable to make (hi ı) kick bout.	تپشدرمم (tĕplshdlrêmĕ) be unable to make (them) kick one another mutually.

PASSIVE.

INTRANSITIVE.

CLASSES.	Determinate.	Indeterminate.	Reciprocal.
Simple	تُبَل (tèpìl) be kicked, be kicked in, &c.	تُبَل (tèpìnl) be kicked about in, &c.	تُبَل (tèpìshìl) be mutually kicked in, &c.
Causative (Permissive)	تُبْدَرَل (tèpdìrìl) be made to be kicked.	تُبْدَرَل (tèpìndìrìl) be made to be kicked about in.	تُبْدَرَل (tèpìshdìrìl) be made to kick mutually one another.
Simple	تُبَلمَ (tèpìlmà) be not kicked.	تُبَلمَ (tèpìnllmà) be not kicked about in.	تُبَلمَ (tèpìshìlmà) be not mutually kicked in.
Causative (Permissive)	تُبْدَرَلمَ (tèpdìrèlmà) be not made to be kicked.	تُبْدَرَلمَ (tèpìndìrìlmà) be not made to be kicked about in.	تُبْدَرَلمَ (tèpìshdìrìlmà) be not made to mutually kick one another.
Simple	تُبَلمَ (tèpìlèmè) be unable to be kicked.	تُبَلمَ (tèpìnlèmè) be unable to e kicked about n.	تُبَلمَ (tèpìshlèmè) be unable to be mutually kicked in.
Causative (Permissive)	تُبْدَرَلمَ (tèpdìrìlèmè) be unable to be made to be kicked.	تُبْدَرَلمَ (tèpìndìrìlèmè) be unable to be made to be kicked about in.	تُبْدَرَلمَ lshdìrìlèmè) be unable to be made to mutually kick one another.

Remarks on the foregoing Table.

The imperative singular is the root, or simplest form in the conjugation, primitive or derivative, of the Turkish verb. This conjugation—unique for all the thirty-six forms, as will be seen further on—consists in adding certain vowels and consonants to the end of this conjugational root.

When the conjugational root of the simple affirmative form ends in ل, or in a vowel, it forms its passive by adding ن instead of ل. Thus : بول (bul) *find,* بولُن (bûlun, the uturu dominating) *be found;* قابلا (qapla) *cover,* قابلان (qaplan) *be covered ;* أوقو (ôqû) *read,* أوقون (ôqun) *be read.* In the foregoing case of the vowel-ending, the passive sometimes takes both the ن and the ل, the ن always preceding ; thus, قابلانل (qaplanîl, as قابلان), *be covered,* أوقونل (oqunul, as أوقون) *be read.*

When the root of the simple affirmative has more than one syllable, and ends in ل, ر, or a vowel, its causative is formed by adding a letter ت in lieu of the syllable در. Thus, قصال (qîsal) *become shorter,* قصالت (qîsalt) *make* or *let* (it) *become shorter; shorten* (it); أوكسور (uksur) *cough,* أوكسورت (uksûrt) *make* or *let* (him) *cough ;* سويله (suweyle) *speak, say,* سويلت (sûweylat) *make* or *let* (him) *speak* or *say, make* or *let* (it) *be spoken* or *said* (by him); أوقو (oqu) *read, recite,* أوقوت (ôqût) *make* or *let* (it) *be read* or *recited* (by him), *make* (him) *read.*

Many simple affirmative verbs ending in consonants also form their causatives in ر, preceded by a servile esere, sometimes written تر, and even ور, with uturu; not in در. No rule appears to exist on this subject, and the dictionary alone, or experience, can help the student in it. Thus, اچ (ích) *drink* (it), اچیر (íchir) or ایچور (íchur) *make* or *let* (it) *be drunk* (by him); نات (bất) *sink* (thou), ناتر (batîr) *make* or *let* (it) *sink, sink* (it); قاچ (qấch) *flee, escape,* قاچر (qấchîr) *make* or *let* (him) *flee* or *escape.*

When the simple verb, affirmative, negative, or impotential, is transitive, its causative governs the same accusative; and the nominative to the simple then becomes a dative to the causative. Thus, بن انی یازدم (ben aní yazdîm) *I wrote it,* سن انی نكا یازدردن (sau aní bana yazdîrdîn) *thou madest it to be written by me* (thou causedst to me the writing it), *thou madest* or *lettest me write it.*

When the simple verb is neuter, its nominative becomes the accusative of its causative; as, اویودم (uyúdum) *I slept,* سن بنی اویوتدن (san benî úyútdun) *thou madest* or *lettest me sleep.*

An indefinite series of causatives of every verb may be formed by repeating the causative suffixes, ت after در, and در after ت. They are sometimes useful, but are generally used in irony; each augment adds an agent to the chain; as, یازمن,

يازِدِرتَدِرمَق , يازِدِرتَمَق , يازِدِرمَق , &c.; this last means *to cause* (a thing) *to be caused* (by a second) *to be caused* (by a third) *to be written* (by a fourth agent).

The indeterminate is also called the *Reflexive* form. It has two uses. More generally it has the same intransitive sig- nification with the simple form, as to the action, but betokens that this action is then performed without any determinate exterior object. Thus تَنمَك is, *to kick one's feet or heels about as one lies or stands* (like a dancer, a man in a passion, a dying animal, &c.); باقِنمَق (baqïnmaq) is, *to look about, here and there, in a perplexed or inquisitive manner;* &c. But, at other times, this form is transitive, and then indicates that the agent is either the direct or indirect object, also, of the action,—that the act is done to or for the agent's self. Thus, قِلِج قوشانمَق (qïlïj qushanmaq) *to gird a sword on to one's self;* اَو ایدِنمَك (ev edïnmek) *to acquire a house for one's self;* قاشِنمَق (qashïnmaq) *to scratch one's self* (with one's nails); کِیِنمَك (gïyïnmek) *to put on one's clothes,* چِزمَه کِیِنمَك (chïzmä gïyïnmek) *to put on boots,* چِزمَهلَرِمی کِیِنَیِم (chïzmalerïmï gïyïneyïm) *let me put on my boots;* &c.

Passive verbs of neuters are *defective;* they are conjugated in the third person singular only, and in inflexions over which person and number exercise no influence. They signify, *to be such that the neutral action takes place in, to, for, by, on account of*, &c. (as expressed), something named, as the act of some or any indeterminate agent. Thus, بویله تپنلمز (buyle tepinilmaz) *the act of kicking about is not thus performed,* بورادَه تَپلمز (burada teplnllmaz) *the act of kicking about is not allowed here;* &c. We have such passive verbs in English; as, *to be slept in, to be fought for;* &c.

The Turkish passive verb always has, inherent in it, the sense of *to be —able.* Thus, كسللر (keslllr) *it is cut* (often), *it will be cut* (then), *it is cuttable* (always); ینمز (yenmaz) *it is not eaten* (as a rule), *it will not be eaten* (then), *it is not eatable* (either now, or by nature).

Section IX. *The Turkish Conjugation.*

All Turkish affirmative verbs, active or passive, transitive or intransitive, are conjugated *in one and the same invariable manner*, modified, as to their servile vowels and consonants, by the laws of class and euphony alone. The negative and impotential verbs differ from the affirmative, as to conjugation, merely in the form of the aorist active participle, and of the analogous aorist tense indicative. So that only one sole conjugation exists, in reality, in the Turkish language.

The conjugation consists of one simple and three complex categories of moods, tenses, numbers, persons, participles, verbal nouns, and gerunds; all four categories, simple and complex, being fundamentally alike, but each modified in a certain special manner, to express a modified variation of the action.

Each category has six moods : the imperative, indicative, necessitative, optative (also subjunctive), conditional, and infinitive.

The imperative mood has one tense, the future.

The indicative has eight tenses, in four pairs ; the present and imperfect ; the aorist and past ; the perfect and pluperfect ; the future and past future.

The necessitative, optative, and conditional, have one pair each, the aorist and past. The infinitive has but one tense, the present.

Each category has five active participles; the present (which is the general active participle, applicable, in one sense, to any time, past, present, or future), the aorist, the past, the perfect, and the future. In Turkish, the present or active, the perfect or passive, are not confused together as in European languages ; each is distinct in form and in sense, and is different from the gerund in form, as it is, in grammar and in sense, different from the verbal noun.

The active participles of the passive verbs denote the direct recipients of the action of verbs transitive ; the passive participles of the same apply to the indirect objects thereof. The active participles of the passives of intransitives denote the

indirect objects of the intransitive action ; the passive participles of such passives are not in use.

Between the five active and two passive participles of each
category, a Turkish conjugation thus furnishes twenty-eight
participles for every verb, primitive or derivative. By the
use of these numerous participles, it entirely avoids all
necessity for a relative pronoun.

The present active participle adds an ustun and the letters
ان, or only the letter ن, to the root that ends in a consonant ;
the aorist adds a vowel and the letters ا., or only the letter ر,
with an ustun, ور with an uturu, and ر only (or sometimes ير)
with an esere, for which no rule can be given ; the past adds
مش (mlsh, mîsh) to all roots, whatever their ending ; as the
perfect adds دك (dik) or دق (dîq). The future adds an ustun
and the letters دحك (ejek) or دحق (âjâq) to consonantal roots,
and ددحاك or نه جق, with ustun, to vowel roots, including the
negatives and impotentials. Thus, تپن (tepan), قران (qîran)
are present active participles; as, تپنن (tepînan), تشن (tepl-
shan), تپلان (tepîlan), تنلان (tepînîlan), and تشلان (tepîshîlan),
are those of the simple affirmative derivatives. The causatives
in در and in درل add the ustun and ان ; while those in ت change
it into د before the letters ان ; thus, تددران (tepdîran), اوتوردان
(ôtûrdân), تپدربلان (tepdîrîlân), &c. ; تپمش (tepmîsh) ; تپدك
(tepdîk) ; تپه جك (tepejek), تپمیه جك (tepmèyejek), تپهمیه جك
(tepdîk) ;

(tepemeyejek), the final ه of the negative particle مه being
elided as useless.

When the root ends with a vowel, as is the case with all
the negatives and impotentials, the syllable يان (yan, yan) is
added in the present participle, the final ه or ى of the root
being suppressed, and by some even the ا; but the و is kept
intact. Thus, قابلايان or قابلايان (qaplayan), تپمه‌ان (tepmeyan),
تپنه‌ميان (tepinemeyan), يوروييان (yuruyan), اوقوييان (oquyan).

The Turkish present active participle, in colloquial language, as a remanet from eastern Turkish, takes after it the
preposition ده de, da, to form an adverb of past or future time;
as, گدنده (gidande) when (I, thou, &c.) went, or shall go.

The aorist active participle, of the same form as the third
person singular of the aorist tense of the indicative, always
ends in a letter ر in affirmatives, and in the syllable مز (maz)
in negatives and impotentials. Thus, تپر (teper), تپمز (tepmaz),
تپه‌مز (tepemez).

In the simple affirmative, the vowel added to the last consonant of the root, to which the final ر is then appended,
cannot be defined by rule. Of course, it must be hard or soft
according to the dominant in the root; but different verbs
have ustun, others esere, others again uturu, for their vowel;
and with the ustun, all hard verbs add ا, as do some soft
verbs; while other soft verbs dispense with this letter. Thus

we have: قيرار (qîrár), ‸دَر (gîder), صانور (sâuur, *vulg.* ɛauîr),
گو (gelur, *vulg.* gelîr), صيرر (sîyîrîr).

The simple reflexive forms its aorist in uturu and ور (generally pronounced as eseré and يِ). The simple reciprocal does
the same. We have, therefore, تَپنور (teplnur, *vulg.* teplnîr),
تَپِشُور (teplshur, *vulg.* teplshîr). All the simple and causative
passives follow this rule; thus, تَـسلـور (tepllur, teplllîr), تِپنلور
(teplnllur, teplulllîr), تَپِشلُور (tèplshllůr, teplshlllîr); تَپدريِنور (tep-
dlrlllr), نَـدربِنُور (teplndlrlllr), تشدريِلُور (teplshdlrlllr). It will
be observed that a vowel ى is intercalated before the ل in
these words. This is a mechanical rule. The preceding ر is
a letter that does not join on to its follower; this is the sole
reason for the addition of that ى, when the following ل has a
vowel. The same rule is applied by many to the ر of the
causative دِ, in like cases; that is, when it has its vowel, as
it always has in the aorist. The words above given may
therefore be written, سشدريِلور , تِپندريِلور , تپدريِلور ; but this has
no effect on the pronunciation.

The aorist passive participle has the same form as the active
perfect, and the future passive is identical in form with the
future active: تدك (tepdlk); تـمـجَك (tepejek).

There are three verbal nouns; the present or general,
formed by adding مه (me, ma) to the root, exactly like the
negative imperative; the perfect, identical in form with the

perfect active and aorist passive participles ; and the future, identical with the two future participles. Thus, تَپْمَه (tepme); تَپْدِك (tepdik); تَپَهجَك (tépèjèk). The form تَپْمَه (tepme) of the present verbal noun is also that of a verbal adjective passive, signifying *done, made, effected as the result of* (the action of the verb) ; thus, تَپْمَه, as such adjective, means *caused by a kick or kicks.*

This derivative of the transitive verb active simple and causative can also take the passive sense ; thus, كَسْمَه (kesme), which naturally means *an act of cutting*, often means also *an act of being cut;* as, كَسْمَهسِى قُولاَیْ (kesmesì qolay) *it is easily cut.* It is also much used as a passive adjective when the verb is transitive ; as, اِينْجَه كَسْمَه تُوتُون (ìnje kesme tutun) *finely cut tobacco;* and as an active adjective when the verb is intransitive ; as, باباَدَنْ قاَلْمَه ماَلْ (babadan qalma mal) *property remaining from* (one's) *father.*

Leaving the gerunds for the present, we may now inquire into the mode of formation of the tenses of each mood. But before doing so, we must indicate the differences that serve clearly to distinguish the active participles, the passive participles, and the verbal nouns, of the two forms in دِك or دِق , and in دَحَلَه or دجق.

In the first place, the participles are adjectives, while the verbal nouns are substantives. Therefore, whenever a derivative in either of those forms qualifies a substantive, it must be a participle; it cannot be a verbal noun.

Secondly, the active participle qualifies the name of its actor only. It is therefore always a simple and invariable word, like the other active participles; as, وارمی ادم تدك اورأیه *is there any man who has gone there?* سین سنمی کَدَه‌دَك *art thou he who is to go?*

Thirdly, the passive participle always qualifies the name of the direct object, or of the indirect object, of the action, and is always accompanied by a possessive pronoun indicating the actor of that action. The first of these two facts distinguishes the passive participle from the verbal noun; the second distinguishes it from the active participle of the same form. Thus, تَاب اوودیعم (oqudughum kĭtāb) *the book which I read* (now or formerly); دتَاب اُوقوبه‌حغَم (ŏquyajaghĭm kĭtab) *the book which I am going to read.* These are instances of the direct object qualified. So, زَمان اُوقودـغَم (oqudughŭm zeman) *the time in which* (i. e. *when*) *I read;* and محلس اوویه‌جغم کتَابى (kĭtābĭ ŏquyajaghĭm mejlĭs) *the meeting in which I am going to read the book,* are instances of indirect objects; as is also اوطه اُوقوبه‌حغَم (uyuyajaghĭm ŏda) *the room in which I am going to sleep.*

As instances of the substantival nature of the verbal nouns, let us take, کُوردُبِكزمى یَردیعم یَازى (yăzĭ yazdĭghĭmĭ gyurdŭnuz-

mu) *have you seen my past action of writing writing?* i. e., *have
you ever seen me write?* كله‌حكمی ده‌یم سونلدی (galejeyïmï kïm
suweyledï) *who mentioned my future action of coming?* i. e., *who
told* (you, him, &c.) *that I was about to come?*

Proceed we now to discuss the formation of the tenses.

The third person singular is the root of each tense, except
in the imperative. Leaving the numbers and persons for
future consideration, we may say, in the first place, that, as
the second tense in each pair, of every mood (excluding the
imperative and the infinitive), is formed from the first tense
of the pair by the addition of the auxiliary ایدی (ïdï) *was*, after
it, we may leave these second tenses also for future con
sideration.

By these means we arrive at the conclusion that there are
four tenses in the indicative, and one each in the necessitative,
optative, conditional, and infinitive, the forms of which have
to be defined.

The four indicative tenses are—the present, the aorist
(present habitual and future promissive), the perfect, and the
future; the single tense of the other three moods is their
aorist (present or future); and that of the infinitive is its
present.

The present indicative adds an esere and the syllable یور
(yor) to the consonantal root; thus, تپیور (teplyor). It indi-

cates a present action (actual or habitual); *he is kicking* (now); *he now habitually kicks.* Add the auxiliary اِدِى to this, تَسُورْ اِدِى (tepíyŏr ĭdĭ), and it forms the imperfect, *he was kicking* (then). A final ت more frequently changes to د; as, كَتْمَك ,كِيدِيُورْ (gĭdĭyŏr); اِيدِيُورْ , اِتْمَكْ (ĕdĭyŏr); &c.

The aorist indicative varies in form of the servile syllable, but always ends in ◌ٓ in the affirmatives, and in ◌ٰٓ (mez, maz) in the negatives and impotentials, being identical with the active aorist participle. It indicates a present *habit* (not a present *action*), or a future *assurance*, a future *promise*, as the context or circumstances may require. Thus, تَپَر (teper) *he kicks; he shall* or *will kick;* قِرَار (qîrar) *he breaks; he shall* or *will break;* يورور (yurur) *he walks; he will walk;* اوقور (oqur) *he reads; he will read;* اصرر (ĭsĭrĭr) *he bites; he will bite;* تَپمز (tepmaz) *he does not kick; he will not kick;* تَپَمز (tepemez) *he cannot kick.* The auxiliary اِدِى, added to this, forms the past tense (showing a past *habit*, or an unfulfilled *condition*); تَپَر اِدِى (teper ĭdĭ) *he used to kick; he would kick* (if he could); *he would have kicked* (had he been able); in which two last senses, the expression is a virtual negative: *he kicks* not, because he is not able; *he did not kick,* because he was not able; تَپمز اِدِى (tepmaz ĭdĭ) *he used not to kick; he would not kick* (if he could); *he would not have kicked* (had he been able); تَپَمز اِيدِى (tepemez ĭdĭ) *he used not to be able to kick; he would not be able to kick* (if so and so) ; *he would not have been able to kick* (had not so and so); &c.

The perfect indicative is formed by adding the syllable دِی (dĭ, dĭ), in all cases, to the root. It is used in a determinate, and also in an indeterminate past sense, referring the action to a given past time, or to all past time. Thus, تَبْدِی (tepdĭ) *he kicked* (then); *he has kicked* (without defining when). Add the auxiliary اِیدِی, and the pluperfect results : تَبْدِی اِیدِی (tepdĭ ĭdĭ), or تَبْدِیدِی (tepdĭdĭ), *he had kicked*; تَمَبْدِی اِیدِی *he had not kicked*; تَمَبْدِی اِیدِی *he had not been able to kick.*

The future indicative is identical in form with the active and passive future participles, and with the future verbal noun. It indicates that the action expressed by the conjugational root is about to take place; thus, تَمَجَك *he is about to kick, he is going to kick;* تَمِیَجَك *he is not going to kick;* تَمَمَجَك *he will not be able to kick.* Add the auxiliary اِیدِی, and the past future results تَمَجَك اِیدِی *he was going to kick,* تَمِیَجَك اِیدِی *he was not going to kick;* تَمَمَجَك اِیدِی *he was unable to be about to kick.* Final ت in the root generally changes to د, and a final vowel requires the addition of a consonant ی : اِیدَهَجَك, بُورُونَهَجَك.

The aorist necessitative is formed by adding the syllables مَلِی (melĭ, malĭ) to the root. It indicates a present duty to perform a future act; and corresponds with our *must* or *ought.*

Thus, تَپْمَلُو *he must kick, he ought to kick;* تَپْمَمَلُو *he must not kick, he ought not to kick;* تَپَمَامَلُو *he ought not to be able to kick.* With the auxiliary اِدِی, we have the past necessitative, تَپْمَلِ اِدِی *he ought to have kicked, he should have kicked;* تَپْمَامَلُو اِیدِی *he ought not to have kicked;* تَپَمَامَلُو اِدِی *he ought not to have been able to kick.*

The aorist optative is formed by adding an ustûn and vowel ه to a consonantal root, or a syllable یَه (yè, ya) to a vowel root. Sometimes ا is used in place of ه. The tense is a quasi-imperative, implying optation, or it is a subjunctive. Thus, تَپَه (tepe) *let him kick, may he kick;* (that) *he may kick;* تِپْمَه (tepmeye, with suppression of the ه of the negation) *let him not kick, may he not kick;* (that) *he may not kick;* نَپَمَمَه (tepemeye) *may he not be able to kick;* (that) *he may not be able to kick.* Add now the auxiliary اِدِی, and we form the past tense, a virtual negative, expressive of regret; thus, تَپَه اِیدِی (tepe ìdì, more frequently written and pronounced تِپَیْدِی tepeydì) *had he kicked, if he had kicked; O that he had kicked;* تَپْمَیِیدِی (tepmeyeydì) *had he not kicked, if he had not kicked; O that he had not kicked;* تَپَمَیِیدِی (tepemeyeydì) *had he not been able to kick, if he had not been able to kick; O that he had not been able to kick.*

The aorist conditional is formed by adding the syllable سَه (se, sà) to any root, consonantal or vowel. This performs the

function of our conjunction *if*, in appearance; but, as اَكَرْ
(eyer), *if*, can be placed before it, it really is a subjunctive
tense-ending. As a present, it admits the possibility of the
action; as a future, it virtually denies the occurrence. Thus,
تَپْسَه (tepse) *if he kick, if he were to kick;* تَپْمَسَه (tepmese, the ی
of negation elided) *if he kick not, were he not to kick;* تَپَمَسَه
(tepemese) *should he not be able to kick.* Sometimes it
is desiderative, *O that he kick!* &c. With ایدی added, we
have the past conditional, which is always a virtual negative.
Thus, تَپْسَیْدِی (tepseydí, for تَپْسَه‌ایدی) *had he kicked, if he had
kicked;* تَپْمَسَیْدِی (tepmeseydí) *had he not kicked;* تَپَمَسَیْدِی
(tepemeseydí) *had he not been able to kick.*

The present of the infinitive is formed by adding مَك (mek)
or مَق (máq) to any root. Thus, تَپْمَك (tepmek) *to kick;* قَاپْلَامَق
(qaplamaq) *to cover.* The negative and impotential are frequently written with ا, and sometimes without a vowel-letter
to end the root; as, تَپْمَمَك, تَپْمَامَك (tepmemek), for تَپْمَمَك;
تَپَمَمَك, تَپَمَامَك (tepememek), for تَپَمَمَك; قَاپْلَامَمَق (qaplamá-
maq), قَاپْلَایَمَامَق (qaplayamámaq). This tense is often rendered
in English by the verbal noun in *-ing;* as, كَتْمَك قَالْمَقْدَن اَولَا
(gltmek qálmáqdan evla) *going is better than staying.* It also
takes the suffix لَك, لِك after it to form an equivalent to our
verbal noun in *-ing;* as, كَتْمَكْلِك *an act of going.*

There are seven *gerunds,* one *gerund-like verbal locution* of

cause, one of verbal proportion, and six to indicate various
times in relation with the action. All of these gerunds and
gerund-like locutions presuppose the occurrence of two actions
expressed in the sentence, one by the gerund, the other by a
subsequent verb. The gerunds are a kind of verbal conjunctions, while the gerund-like locutions are verbal adverbs.

The first gerund, the most frequently used, ends in an
uturu, followed by وبْ (ub, ub) after a consonant, or by يوبْ
(yub, yub) after a vowel. It indicates that two actions are
being mentioned, of which the one implied by the gerund is
prior as to time or natural sequence. We more usually, in
English, express this relation of two actions by the conjunction *and*, though we occasionally use our gerund in -*ing*,
as the Turkish does. Thus, تپوبْ قيرار (tepub qîrar) *he kicks
and breaks, will kick and break* (it); or, *kicking* (it), *he will
break* (it). Conversationally, this gerund is pronounced with
eseré in lieu of uturu; and with *p* in place of بْ; as, teplp,
qîrîp, &c.

The second gerund is formed by adding ustun, and the
letters رَكْ (erek) or رَقْ (araq), to a consonantal root, يَرَكْ (yerek)
or يَرَقْ (yaraq) to a vowel-root. It is sometimes used in lieu
of the first gerund, to obviate its too frequent recurrence; but
its distinctive use is to indicate that, of two contemporary
sustained actions expressed, the one, subsidiary, accompanies
the other. Thus, سَرَكْ كَتْدى *kicking, he went off*; i. e., *he*

went off, kicking away (all the time); کولەرَك کلدی *he came, laughing* (all the time).

The third gerund, in ـجَه (ĭnje, ĭnja), after a consonant, or یِنجَه (yĭnje, yĭnja) after a vowel, and the fourth (used in writing only, and much more rarely), in حَاک (ĭjek) or حَق (ĭjaq) after a consonant, یِجَک! (yījèk) or یِجَق (yĭjaq) after a vowel, has the sense that its action is to be a kind of signal for the occurrence of the other expressed in the sentence; it may, then, be rendered by our *on ...* (with a gerund), also by our *as soon as ...* (with a verb). Thus, کورُنجَه تَدی (gyŭrunjè tepdĭ) *on seeing* (him), *he kicked* (him); وَاصلْ اولِجَق مَعلوْ اولَه (vasĭl ŏlījaq, ma'lum ŏla) *on reaching* (as soon as it reaches), *be (it) known (that......)*.

The fifth gerund is identical in form with the aorist optative, repeated. It expresses repetition of one act as a means to the performance of a second. Thus, تَه تَه قیردی (tepe tepe qĭrdĭ), *kicking, (and) kicking* (it), *he broke* (it).

The sixth gerund is the infinitive with esere and نْ added; the Persian ک softened into Turkish ک (*y* value), and the ق into ج. It expresses the verbal reason precedent for the second action. Thus, اُو تَ. کین بَنْ قَاجْدِم *he kicking, I fled*; i. e., *because he kicked, I fled*.

The seventh gerund expresses the beginning of a time commencing with the occurrence of an action and lasting until

now, during which another action has repeatedly or con-
tinuously occurred; it is equivalent to our *ever since* .....
In form it is the fifth gerund (not repeated) with the syllable
لُو (lù) or لِى (lì) added to it. Thus, تَدهِلُو اَقْصَايُورْ (tepelu aqsayor)
ever since he kicked, he has limped.

The causal gerund-like locution is equivalent to the sixth
gerund in sense. It is the infinitive, with its final consonant
softened down, and with the preposition اِلّه (ïle, îla) added,
and shortened into لِ (le, la). Thus, سَمَكْلِه (tepmeyle) *by kicking.* No agent of the verb is then expressed in the verb,
though it be so exteriorly; as, بَنْ تَمَكْلِه *by my kicking, I kicking.* There is another form into which this idea is cast, and
in which a perfect verbal noun, with a suffixed possessive pronoun indicative of the agent, and the ablative preposition دَنْ
(dan) are employed. Thus, تَ. دِيكَ. دَنْ (tepdïylmdan) *by my
(past) act of kicking.* This pronoun varies as is required:
تَبْدِيكَكَدَنْ (tepdïylndan) *by thy act of kicking;* &c.

The gerund-like locution of verbal, i. e., of actional proportion is formed of the perfect active participle, with the
adverbial suffix of manner, جَه (je, jä), added to it. It defines
a duration of time for two concurrent actions, the first circum-
scribing that duration for the continued or repeated occurrence
of the other; as, بَنْ تَبْدِكَه سَنْ طُوت (bén tepdïkje, san tut) *while
I kick, so long as I kick, do thou hold* (him). It sometimes

I

expresses the rate (proportion) of rapidity of the two actions; as, وَقْت كُحدكَه ابرِبَاشُور (waqt gechdĭkje, ĭrĭleshĭr) *as time goes by, it grows large* (larger).

The six verbal times indicated, in reference to an action, are the following: 1, the time before the action; 2, the time when the action is just about to occur; 3, the time while the action occurs; 4, the time when it occurred; 5, the time just when it has occurred; 6, the time after its occurrence. The first is the present verbal noun in the ablative; as, تَمَددَن (tep-medeu), to which, for precision's sake, the adverb اوَّل (avval) or مَقَدَّم (muqaddam), *anteriorly*, is subjoined. The expression تَمَددَن اوَّل (or تَمَددَن اوَّل), then, means *anteriorly to* (earlier than) *the action of kicking*; i. e., *before kicking*. Sometimes this is vulgarly expressed as تَيمزدن اوَّل *before* (the agent) *kicks not;* i. e., *while* (as yet) *he has* (or *had*) *not kicked*.

The second gerund-like locution of time is the future active participle with the auxiliary gerund ايكَن (ĭken), *during*, added to it; thus, سدحك ايكَن *during* (the time of being) *about to kick;* i. e., *when just about to kick*.

The third is the aorist active participle with the same addition: تبر ايكَن *during* (the time of being) *kicking;* i. e., *while kicking*.

The fourth is the perfect verbal noun or active participle, put in the locative (of time). It may be used impersonally,

with no addition in it ; and it may be used, for precision, with
the possessive pronoun of the agent between the verbal noun
and the preposition. In the former case, the verbal derivative
is possibly a participle ; in the latter, it is doubtlessly the
verbal noun. Thus, تپدکده بن *when I* (became) *one who has
kicked* ; or تپدکمده بن *when I* (performed) *my* (past) *act of
kicking* ; i. e., *when I kicked.*

The fifth is the past active participle with the auxiliary
اسكن ; as, یمش ایکن *during* (this time of the condition of)
having kicked; i.e., *now that kicking has occurred, since (I, &c.)
have kicked.*

The sixth is the perfect verbal noun in the ablative (of
time), followed by the adverb صكره (sónra, sora), *after ·* thus,
تپدکدن صكره (tepdíkdan sóra) *after the act of kicking.* The
possessive pronouns may be introduced into this locution before
the preposition ; as, تپدیکمدن صكره (tepdíylmdan sóra) *after
my action of kicking.*

SECTION X. *The Numbers and Persons of the Verb.*

In all the tenses the first person singular is expressed by
the personal suffix م added to the verb, with eseré given to the
tense-root, when this is a consonant ; and suppressing the final
ى of the tense-root where it occurs ; adding one where wanted.

It is wanting in the imperative. Thus : تپــيــورم (teplyorìm) *I am kicking* ; تپیور ایدم (teplyor-ìdìm) *I was kicking* ; تپرم (teperìm) *I kick ; I shall* or *will kick* ; تپر ایدم (teper-ìdìm) *I used to kick ; I would kick ; I would have kicked;* تپدم (tepdìm) *I kicked ; I did kick ; I have kicked* ; تپدیدم (tepdìdìm) or تپدم ایدی (tepdìm-ìdì) *I had kicked;* تپهجكم (tepejeyìm) *I am going to kick;* تپهجكدم (tepejekdìm) *I was going to kick ;* تپملویم (tepmellyìm) *I must kick;* تپ ملو ایدم (tepmell-ìdìm) *I should have kicked, ought to have kicked;* تپهدم (tepem) *that I may kick;* تپهیدم (tepeydìm) *that I had kicked ;* تپسهم (tepsem) *if I kick ;* تسهدم (tepseydìm) *if I had kicked.*

The second person singular, in all the tenses in ی د, is formed by changing the vowel ی into the nasal Turkish ك ; as, تپیور ایدك (teplyòr-ìdìn), تپر ایدك (teper-ìdìn), تپدك (tepdìn), تپهجك ایدك (tepejek-ìdìn), تپملو ایدك (tepmell-ìdìn), تپهیدك (tepey- dìñ), تپسهدك (tepseydìn). All the other tenses form it in سین (sìn), sometimes written and pronounced سك (sìn), excepting the present of the conditional, which forms it with سهك (san, san) ; sometimes written سَك, but pronounced like سَهك. Thus, تپیورسین (teplyòrsìu), تپرسین (tepersìu), تپهجكسین (tepejeksìn) ; تپملوسین (tepmellsìu), تپهسین (tepesìu).

The first person plural, likewise, in all the tenses in ی د, is

formed by changing the vowel ى into Arabic ك (*k* value) ;
excepting that of the perfect, which, in hard words, always
forms this person in ق instead of ك. Thus, تَمُوْ اٮدك (teplyór-
ldík), تٟبَّر ايدك (teper-ídík), تمدك (tépdík), تددٮدك (tepdídík, or
تٟمدك ايدى tepdík-ídí), تمجك ايدك (tépéjek-ídík, or
تٟمٟحٟكدك tepejeyídík, or تٟمٟحٟكدك tepejekdík), تمماٯ ايدك (tepmell-ídík),
تٟمٟدك (tepeydík), تٟمٟمدك (tepseydík). With a hard word like
ٮانمق (baqmaq), the perfect forms ٮاقدق (báqdíq). If this person in the past future indicative, in the past optative, and in
the past conditional, is used in the contracted form, these also,
with hard words, use ق instead of ك ; as, ٮاقمجٟغدق (baqajagh-
díq), ٮاقٮدق (baqaydíq), ٮاقٮسدق (baqsaydíq). In the imperative
and present optative, it is formed by adding ústun and لـ to
the consonantal root, the syllable لـ having esere for its vowel ;
or, in vowel-roots, by adding the two syllables ٮٟلـ (yelím,
yalím) ; thus, تمٟلـ (tépelím), ٮاقٟلٟم (báqálím), سُوٮلٟمٟلٟم (súwey-
leyelím), اوُٯُوٮٟٮٟلٟم (óqúyalím, for اوُٯُوٮٟٮٟلٟم). In hard words, the
present of the conditional forms this person with ق also ; as,
ٮاقسٯ (baqsaq, sometimes written ٮاقسق), اوٯوسٟمدق (oqúsaq,
اوٯٯوسٟٯ). The present, aorist, and future indicative, with the
present necessitative, form it in ز or ٮز, with esere added to
the final consonant of the tense-root of the indicatives, and
with that vowel given to the ى of ٮز in the necessitative ;

thus, تپورز (teplyórïz), برز (tepérïz), تمه‌حکـز (tepejeyïz, the Arabic ك changed into Turkish ك, y value), تَمْلوُنْز (tepme-llyïz). In hard words, the future indicative is in ج (softened ق), with esere before the final ز ; as, ناقه‌حغز (baqajaghïz).

The second person plural, again, in all the tenses in دی, is formed in دیکز (dïñïz ; which is hard in the perfect of hard words, dïnïz). Thus, تسورردیدز (teplyordïnïz), تردیکز (teper-dïñïz), تَپْدیکِز (tépdïñïz), باقْدیکِز (báqdïñïz), تَپْدیدیکِز (tépdï-dïñïz), تَپمَلل‌ایدیکز (tépméll-ïdïñïz), تَمَحَکْدیکِز (tépéjéydïñïz), تَپیْدیکِز (tepeydïnïz), تِپَسَیْدیکِز (tepseydïnïz). The imperative has two forms, in ك and in كز, both preceded by esere, and a consonant ی in vowel-roots ; as, تـك (tepïn), بـكز (tepïnïz, written also تَـپـكـز) ; ناك (baqïn), ناتـكـز (baqïnïz); قـالّاك (qaplayïn), اوقونـكـز (oquyunuz ; the uturu dominating). All the other tenses form it in سـكـز (sïñïz, sïnïz), except the present conditional, which has ustun for its first vowel, often written سـكـز (sanïz, sanïz, to distinguish it better). Thus, تِیوُرسِكِز (teplyórsïñïz), تَپِرْسِکـز (tépérsïñïz), تَمَحَکْسِکـز (tépéjék-sïnïz ; hard in hard words, تَمْلوُسَکـز ناقه‌حقْسَکـز baqajaqsïnïz), (tepmellsïnïz), نیه‌سکـز (tepesïnïz ; hard in hard words, ناه‌سکز baqasïnïz), تَسَه‌كـز (tepsenïz; hard in hard words, ناقْسَه‌دز baqsanïz).

The third person plural is formed from the same person of

the singular, with the syllable لر (ler, lar) added. Thus, تِپسُونْلَر
(tėpsinlėr); تِپيُورْلَر (tėplyórlår), تَپِرْلَر (tėpėrlėr), تِپْدِيلَر (tėpdilėr),
تِپَهجَكْلَر (tėpėjėklėr), تِپْمَلِيلَر (tėpmėlilėr), تِپَهلَر (tėpėlėr), تِپْسَهلَر
(tepseler). The tenses in ابدِی may be formed in this way,
ابدِی becoming ابدلَر (idiler); *or*, the plural sign may be given
to the radical element, and ايدِی be kept unchanged; as,
بِيُورْرَ ,يدَی or بِيُورْ ايديلَر; and so throughout, except the past
optative, which prefers دلَر.

SECTION XI. *Of the Complex Categories.*

The Complex Categories of every Turkish verb, active or
passive, transitive or intransitive, affirmative, negative, or impotential, are formed, even as to their roots, with an auxiliary
verb, أُولَـمَق (ólmaq) *to be or become;* itself conjugated, as a
simple verb, in conformity with what has already been laid
down, and joined to the aorist, past, and future active participles of the verb of which the complex category is to be
formed. The auxiliary follows the participle.

With the aorist participle, the auxiliary verb أُولَ . ق forms
the First Complex Category; with the past participle, it forms
the Second Complex Category; and with the future participle,
it forms the Third Complex Category.

It would be possible to avoid using these terms, and to fuse

the whole into one vast conjugation, by following the method
used by European grammarians, each for the European language in which he treats of the subject. In some respects,
such an arrangement would possess an advantage. It would
bring together tenses of the one verb, which are but delicate
modifications of each other. The disadvantage would be, on
the whole, preponderant; for the one vast conjugation of
simple and complex tenses formed with continually inter-
mingling, varying participles, would be very puzzling to the
novice, would choke out of view the principles of the subdivision, and prevent a lucid exposition thereof, besides
demanding the invention of a host of new names by which
to distinguish the numerous tenses so brought together;
whereas, by keeping the same names for the same tenses of
the four categories, it would seem that a truer perception
of the shade of meaning which distinguishes each of the four
tenses of each name will be more easily attained and more
firmly grasped. Still, as a comparison with other systems
offers a certain amount of utility, we have given below the
three complex categories apart, to show their principles, and
have then arranged the whole four categories as a single conjugation.

SECTION XII. *The First Complex Category.*

This is formed with the aorist active participle, of every

class of verb, active or passive, transitive or intransitive, primary or derivative, affirmative or negative. In form, it is simply the conjugation of the auxiliary verb اولمق (ŏlmaq) *to be*, the participle, as an adjective, remaining invariable throughout. We give one person only in each tense.

Infinitive.

تَپَرَاوُلْمَقْ (teper olmaq)   To be a willing, natural, deter-
         mined, constant, or habitual
         kicker ; to be kicking ; to
         kick (habitually).

Imperative.

تَپَرَاوُلْ (teper ŏl)   Be thou kicking ; kick thou
         (habitually).

Indicative.

Present.

تَپَرَاوُلِيُورِمْ (teper ŏllyŏrîm)   I am continually kicking.

Imperfect.

تَپَرَاوُلِيُورْ ايِدِمْ (teper ŏllyŏr ĭdĭm) I was continually kicking.

Aorist.

تَپَرَاوُلُرُمْ (teper olurum)   I am continually kicking ; I
         shall be ever kicking.

Past.

تَپَرَاوُلُرْ ايِدِمْ (teper ŏlur ĭdĭm)   I used to be always kicking ;
         I would be, *or* would have
         been, always kicking.

Perfect.

تپر اولدم (teper oldum)   I became a constant kicker.

Pluperfect.

تپر اولدم ایدی (teper oldŭm ĭdĭ)   I had been or become a constant kicker.

Future.

تپر اوله‌جغم (teper olajaghĭm)   I am about to become a constant kicker.

Future Past.

تپر اوله‌جغیم (teper ŏlajaghdĭm)   I was about to become a constant kicker.

Necessitative.

Aorist.

تپر اولملویم (teper ŏlmalĭyĭm)   I must be, or become, a constant kicker.

Past.

تپر اولملو ایدم (teper ŏlmalĭyĭdĭm)   I ought to have been a constant kicker.

Optative.

Aorist.

تپر اوله‌دم (teper olayĭm)   That I may be a constant kicker.

Past.

تپر اولدم (teper olaydĭm)   That I had been a constant kicker.

Conditional.

Aorist.

تَپَرْ اُولْسَمْ (teper ölsam)   Were I, should I become, a constant kicker.

Past.

تپر اولسدم، (teper ölsaydĭm)   Had I been a constant kicker.

Active Participles.

Present.

تپر اولان (teper ölan)   Who *or* which is, was, will be, a constant kicker.

Aorist.

تَپَرْ اُولُور (teper ölür)   (*perhaps unused, as a cacophony.*)

Past.

تپر اولمش (teper olmush)   Who has been a constant kicker.

Perfect.

تپر اولدق (teper oldŭq)   Who was a constant kicker.

Future.

تـ اولهجق (teper ölajaq)   Who is to be a constant kicker.

Passive Participles.

Aorist.

تَپَرْ اُولدق (teper ölduq)   Who *or* which (a kicker) has constantly kicked.

Future.

تپر اولَجَق (teper ólajaq)   Who, which (I, &c.) am about
constantly to kick.

Verbal Nouns.

Present.

تپر اولمه (teper olma)   The act of being (at any time)
a constant kicker.

Perfect.

تپر اولدق (teper ólduq)   The act of having been (then)
a constant kicker.

Future.

تپر اولَجق (teper olajaq)   The act of being about (now)
to become (hereafter) a con-
stant kicker.

Gerunds.

1st.   تپر اولوب (teper ólúp)   Being a constant kicker
(and ......).

2nd.   تپر اولَرق (teper olaraq)   Continuing to be a constant kicker (*so and so
also occurs*).

3rd.   تپر اولنجه (teper olunjå)   ⎰ As soon as —— becomes
(became, will become) a
4th.   تپر اويجَق (teper olıjaq)   ⎱ constant kicker, ...

5th. تَرَ اوله اوله (teper ӧla ӧla)   By continually being a con-
                                      stant kicker, ...

6th. تَرَّ اولْمَغِن (teper olmaghin)   By reason of being a con-
                                      stant kicker, ...

7th. تَرَ اولَلِى (teper olalĭ)   Ever since —— became
                                (has been) a constant
                                kicker, ...

Section XIII.   *The Second Complex Category.*

Infinitive.

Present.

تَمْش أُولِمَق (tepmlsh ӧlmaq)   To have kicked.

Imperative.

Future.

تَمْش أُول (tepmlsh ӧl)   Be thou one who has
                              kicked ; have kicked.

Indicative.

Present.

تَمْش أُولِيُورِم (tepmlsh ӧllyӧrĭm)   I am, *or* am becoming, one
                                     who has kicked; I have
                                     kicked.

Imperfect.

سَمْش أُولِيُورْدِ (tepmlsh ӧllyӧrdĭm)   I was, *or* was becoming,
                                       one who has kicked.

Aorist.

تَمْش أُولُورِم (tepmlsh ӧlŭrum)   I shall have kicked.

Past

تَپمِش اُولُورْدُم (tepmlsh olurdum)   I should have kicked.

Perfect.

تَپمِش اُولْدُم (tepmlsh óldum)   I became one who had kicked, I had kicked.

Pluperfect.

تَپمِش اُولْدُم اِیدِى (tepmlsh oldum ldl)   I had become one who has kicked.

Future.

تَپمِش اُولَجَغِم (tepmlsh olajaghlm)   I am about becoming one who has kicked; I am going to have kicked.

Future Past.

تَپمِش اُولَجَّقّ اِیدِم (tèpmlsh óläjäq ldlm)   I was about to have kicked.

Necessitative.

Aorist.

تَپمِش اُولْمَلِیِم (tepmlsh ólmallylm)   I must (now) have kicked (then).

Past.

تَپمِش اُولْمَلِو اِیدِم (tepmlsh ólmally ldlm)   I must (then) have (already) kicked (before).

Optative.

Aorist.

تَپمِش اُولَه‌یِم (tèpmlsh ólaylm, اولاهم ólam)   That I may have kicked.

Past.

تَپْمِش اُولَيْدِم (tĕpmĭsh ŏlắydĭm)   That I had kicked.

Conditional.
Aorist.

تَمِش اُولْسَم (tepmĭsh ŏlsam, اولسم) Had I kicked (then).

Past.

تَمِش اُلْسَیْدِم (tepmĭsh olsaydĭm)   Had I (already) kicked (before then).

Active Participles.
Present.

تَپْمِش اُولَان (tepmĭsh ŏlan)   Who has (already) kicked.

Aorist.

تَمِش اُولُور (tepmĭsh ŏlur)   Who will have (already) kicked.

Past *and* Perfect, *perhaps not used.*

Future.

تَمِش اُولَهجَق (tepmĭsh olajaq)   Who will become one who has kicked.

Passive Participles.
Aorist.

تَمِش اُولْدُق (tepmĭsh ŏldŭq)   Which (a kicker) had (already) kicked.

Future.

تَپْمِشْ اُولَجَقْ (tepmish ólajaq)   Which (a kicker) will have kicked.

Verbal Nouns.

Present.

تَپْمِشْ اُولْمَه (tepmish olma)   The (present state of) having (already) kicked.

Perfect.

تَپْمِشْ اُولْدُقْ (tepmish oldúq)   The (past state of) having (previously) kicked.

Future.

تَپْمِشْ اُولَجَقْ (tépmish ólájáq)   The (future state of) having (previously) kicked.

Gerunds.

1st. تَپْمِشْ اُولُوبْ (tépmish ólup)   Having kicked (and....).

2nd. اُولَرَقْ ... (... oláraq)   Having the continued quality of having kicked (and ...).

3rd. اُولِنْجَه ... (... olúnja)   As soon as (— is, was, will be) one who *or* which had kicked, ...

4th. اُولِيجَقْ ... (... ólijaq)   The instant (—) had kicked, ...

5th. تپمش اوله اوله (tepmĭsh olā ŏla) By continuing to have kicked, ...

6th. اولمغین ... (... olmaghĭn) By reason of having kicked, ...

7th. اولدلی ... (... ŏlalĭ) Since — became one who had kicked, ...

SECTION XIV. *The Third Complex Category.*

Infinitive.
Present.

تپه‌جك اولمق (tepejek olmaq) To be about to kick (ready to kick).

Imperative.
Future.

تپه‌جك اول (tepeɟek ŏl) Be thou about to kick.

Indicative.
Present.

تپه‌جك اولیورم (tepejek ŏlĭyŏrĭm) I am (often) on the point of kicking; I become on the point ....

Imperfect.

تپه‌جك اولیور ایدم (tĕpĕjĕk ŏlĭyor ĭdĭm) I was (often) on the point ....

Aorist.

تپه‌جك اولورم (tĕpejek ŏlŭrŭm) I am (habitually), I shall be (then) on the point ...

Past.

تپه‌جك اُولُوردُم (tepejek ŏlurdum) — I used (habitually); I should be (then) ou the point ....

Perfect.

تپه‌جك اُولدُم (tepejek ŏldum) — I was (then) on the point ....

Pluperfect.

تپه‌جك اُولدُم ایدی (tepejek oldum ĭdĭ) — I had been (before then) on the point ....

Future *and* Future Past.

تپه‌جك اُوله‌جغم (tėpėjėk ŏlåjåghĭm) ⎫
تپه‌جك اُوله‌جغدم (tėpėjėk ŏlåjåghdĭm) ⎬ *Not used, as being cacophonies.*

Necessitative.

Aorist.

تپه‌حك اُولمَلُویم (tepejek ŏlmalîyĭm) — I must be on the point ....

Past.

تپه‌حك اُولمَلُو ایدم (tepejek ŏlmålîyĭdĭm) — I ought to have been on the point ....

Optatıve.

Aorist.

سَده‌جك اُوله‌م (tepejek olam) — That I may be on the point ....

Past.

تَپِه جَكْ اُولَيـْدِمْ (tèpéjek òlaydìm)   That I had been on the point ....

Conditional.

Aorist.

تَمَه حَكْ اُولْسَه (tepejek olsam)   Were I to be *or* become on the point ....

Past.

تَپِه جَكْ اُولْسَيـْدِمْ (tepejek òlsaydìm)   Had I been on the point ....

Active Participles.

Present.

بَيَه حَكْ اُولَانْ (tepejek òlan)   Who *or* which is *or* becomes on the point ....

Aorist.

تَپِه جَكْ اُولُورْ (tepejek òlùr)   Who *or* which is (naturally) *or* will be (some time) on the point ....

Past *and* Perfect.

تَپِه جَكْ اُولْمُشْ (tèpèjèk òlmùsh)   }
تَپِه جَكْ اُولْدُقْ (tèpèjèk òldùq)   }   Who *or* which has been *or* was (then) on the point....

Future.

تَپِه حَكْ اولَه حَ (tèpejek òlajaq)   *Not used, as being cacophonous.*

Passive Participles.

Aorist.

تَمَحَك اولدق (tepejek oldúq)   Which (a kicker) was on the point ....

Future.

Cacophonous; not used.

Verbal Nouns.

Present.

تَمَحَك اولمه (tèpèjèk olma)   The act of being *or* becoming (at any time) on the point....

Perfect.

تَپَجَك اُولْدُق (tepejek ólduq)   The past act *or* state of being (then) on the point ....

Future.

Cacophonous; not used.

Gerunds.

1st. تَمَحَك اُولـوبْ (tepejek ólúp)   Being about to kick (and ....)

2nd. اُولَرَق ... (... olaraq)   Continuing to be about to kick (and ....)

3rd. اُوَّتَه أُو ... (... olúnja)   As soon as (— is, was, will be) about to kick, ...

4th. اولِيَى ... *Cacophonous.*

5th. تَپَجَكْ اُولَه اُولَه (tèpèjèk ólå ólå) By continuing to be about to kick, ...

6th. اُولْمَغِين (...) ... ólmåghìn) By reason of being about ....

7th. اُولَـهلِی (...) ... ólålì) Ever since — became on the point ....

Section XV. *The Combined (true Turkish) Conjugation.*

Infinitive.

Present.	تَپْمَكْ	تَپْراوُاَق	تَپْمِش اُولْمَق	پَهجَكْ اُولْمَق

Imperative.

Future.	تَپْ	تَپْراوُلْ	تَپْمِش اُولْ	پَهجَكْ اُولْ

Indicative.

Present.	تَپِيُورْ	تَپْراوُلِيُورْ	تَپْمِش اُولِيُورْ	پَهجَكْ اُولِيُورْ
Imperf.	تَپِيُورْدِی	اُولِيُورْدِی ...	... اُولِيُورْدِی	... اُولِيُورْدِی
Aorist.	تَپَرْ	اُولُورْ ...	... اُولُورْ	... اُولُورْ
Past.	تَپَرْدِی	اُولُورْدِی ...	... اُولُورْدِی	... اُولُورْدِی
Perfect.	تَپْدِی	اُولْدِی ...	... اُولْدِی	... اُولْدِی
Pluperf.	تَپْدِیدِی	اُولْدِیدِی ...	... اُولْدِیدِی	... اُولْدِیدِی
Future.	تَپَهجَكْ	اُولَهجَقْ ...	... اُولَهجَقْ	(*not used*)
Fut.Past.	تَپَهجَكْدِی	اُولَهجَقْدِی	... اُولَهجَقْدِی	(*not used*)

Necessitative.

| Aorist. | تَپَمْلِو | تَپَرْ اُولْمَلِو | تَپْمِش اُولْمَلِو | تَپَه‌جَك اُولْمَلِو |
| Past. | تَپْ۔۔۔وايدی | ۔۔۔ اُولْمَلِوايدی | ۔۔۔ اُولْمَلِوايدی | ۔۔۔ اُولْمَلِوايدی |

Optative.

| Aorist. | تَپَه | تَرَ اُولَه، | تَمِش، اُولَه | تَپَه‌جَك اُولَه |
| Past. | تَپَیْدی | ۔۔۔ اُولَیْدی | ۔۔۔ اُولَیْدی | ۔۔۔ اُولَیْدی |

Conditional.

| Aorist. | تَپْسَه | تَپَرْ اُولْسَه | تَپْمِش اُولْسَه - | پَه‌جَك اُولْسَه |
| Past. | تَپْسَیْدی | ۔۔۔ اُولْسَیْدی | ۔۔۔ اُولْسَیْدی | ۔۔۔ اُولْسَیْدی |

Active Participles.

Present. (تَان) تَپَن	تَپَرْ اُولَان	تَپْمِش اُولَان	پَه‌جَك اُولَان
Aorist.	تَپَرْ	۔۔۔ اُولُورْ	۔۔۔ اُولُورْ	۔۔۔ اُولُورْ
Past.	تَپْمِش	۔۔۔ اُولْمِش	(not used)	۔۔۔ اُولْمِش
Perfect.	تَپْدِك	۔۔۔ اُولْدُقْ	۔۔۔ اُولْدُقْ	۔۔۔ اُولْدُقْ
Future.	تَپَه‌جَك	۔۔۔ اُولَه‌جَقْ	۔۔۔ اُولَه‌جَقْ	(not used)

Passive Participles.

| Aorist. | تَپْدِك | تَپَرْ اُولْدُقْ | تَپْمِش اُولْدُقْ | پَه‌جَك اُولْدُقْ |
| Future. | تَپَه‌جَك | ۔۔۔ اُولَه‌جَقْ | ۔۔۔ اُولَه‌جَقْ | (not used) |

Verbal Nouns.

Present.	تَپْمَه	تَپْرَاوْلْمَه	تَپْمِش اوْلْمَه	تَپَهجَكْ اوْلْمَه
Perfect.	تَپْدِكْ	...اوُلْدُقْ	...اوْلْدُقْ	...اوْلْدُقْ
Future.	تَپَهجَكْ	...اوُلَهجَقْ	...اوْلَهجَقْ	(*not used.*)

...   ...*Gerunds.* . .

1st.	تَپُوبْ	تَپْرَاوْلُوبْ	تَپْمِش اوْلُوبْ	تَپَهجَكْ اوْلُوبْ
2nd.	تَپَرَكْ	...اوُلَهرَقْ	...اوْلَهرَقْ	...اوْلَهرَقْ
3rd.	تَپْنْجَـه	...اوُلْنْجَـه	...اوْلْنْجَـه	...اوْلْنْجَه
4th.	تَپِيجَكْ	...اوُلِيجَقْ	...اوْلِيجَقْ	...اوْلِيجَقْ
5th.	تَپَه تَپَه	...اوُلَه اوُلَه	...اوْلَه اوْلَه	...اوْلَه اوْلَه
6th.	تَپْمَكِـين	...اوُلْمَغِين	...اوْلْمَغِين	...اوْلْمَغِين
7th.	تَپَهلِو	...اوُلَهلِو	...اوْلَهلِو	...اوْلَهلِو

Section XVI. *The Negative and Impotential Conjugations.*

The Negative and Impotential Conjugations, twenty-four in
number to each simple verb, as a general rule, are formed precisely on the lines of the simple affirmative conjugation in its
four categories, as above given, with the exception of the
aorist of the indicative, as to its root-word of the third person

singular, and the corresponding aorist active participle, which end in مَزْ (maz), instead of the final ر of the affirmative.

Infinitive.

Present.

تَپَمَكْ	تَپْمَزْ اُولْمَقْ	تَپَامِشْ اُولْمَقْ	تَپْمَیَهجَكْ اُولْمَقْ
تَپَمَامَكْ	تَپَمَزْ ...	تَپَمَامِشْ ...	تَپَمَیَهجَكْ ...

Imperative.

Future.

تَپْمَه	تَپْمَزْ اُولْ	تَپَامِشْ اُولْ	تَپْمَیَهجَكْ اُولْ
تَپَهمَه	تَپَمَزْ ...	تَپَمَامِشْ ...	تَپَمَیَهجَكْ ...

Indicative.

Present.

تَپْمِیُورْ	تَپْمَزْ اُولِیُورْ	تَپَامِشْ اُولِیُورْ	تَپْمَیَهجَكْ اُولِیُورْ
تَپَمِیُورْ	تَپَمَزْ ...	تَپَمَامِشْ ...	تَپَمَیَهجَكْ ...

Imperfect.

تَپْمِیُورْدِی	تَپْمَزْ اُولِیُورْدِی	تَپَامِشْ اُولِیُورْدِی	تَپْمَیَهجَكْ اُولِیُورْدِی
تَپَمِیُورْدِی	تَپَمَزْ ...	تَپَمَامِشْ ...	تَپَمَیَهجَكْ ...

Aorist.

Past.

تَمِيَهجَك اُولُورْدُی   تَمَاشْ اُولُورْدُی   تَمْز اُولُورْدُی   تَمْزْدِی

تَپَمِيَهجَك ...   تَپَمَامِشْ ...   تَپَمَزْ ...   تَپَهمَزْ:

Perfect.

تَمِيَهجَك اُولْدُی   تَمَاشْ اُولْدُی   تَمْز اُولْدُی   تَمْدِی

تَپَمِيَهجَك ...   تَپَمَامِشْ ...   تَپَهمَزْ ...   تَپَهمَدِی

Pluperfect.

تَمِيَهجَك اُولْدِيدِی   تَمَاشْ اُولْدِيدِی   تَمْز اُولْدِيدِی   تَمْدِيدِ

تَپَمِيَهجَك ...   تَپَمَامِشْ ..   تَپَهمَزْ ...   تَپَهمَدِ

Future.

(*not used*)   تَمَاشْ اُولَهجَقْ   تَمْز اُولَهجَقْ   تَمِيَهج

(*not used*)   تَپَمَامِشْ ...   تَپَهمَزْ ...   تَپَهمِيَه

Future Past.

(*not used*)   تَمَاشْ اُولَهجَقْدِی   تَمْز اُولَهجَقْدِی   تَمِيَهج

(*not used*)   تَپَمَامِشْ ...   تَپَهمَزْ ...   تَپَهمِيَه:

Necessitative.

Aorist.

تَمِيَهجَك اُولْمَلِو   تَمَاشْ اُولْمَلِو   تَمْز اُولْمَلِو   تَمَامْلِو

Past.

تَمَامْلُو ايدى	تَمَامِش اُولْمَلُو ايدى	تَمِزْ اُولْمَلُو ايدى	تَمِيَهجَكْ اُولْمَلُو ايدى
تَپَمَامَلُو ايدى	تَپَمَامِش ...	تَپَمَزْ ...	تَپَمِيَهجَكْ ...

Optative.
Aorist.

تَمِيَه	تَمِزْ اُوله	تَمَامِش اُوله	تَمِيَهجَكْ اُوله
تَپَمَيَه	تَپَمَزْ ...	تَپَمَامِش ...	تَپَمِيَهجَكْ ...

Past.

تَمِيدى	تَمِزْ اُولَيْدى	تَمَامِش اُولَيْدى	تَمِيَهجَكْ اُولَيْدى
تَپَمَييدى	تَپَمَزْ ...	تَپَمَامِش ...	تَپَمِيَهجَكْ ...

Conditional.
Aorist.

تَمِسَه	تَمِزْ اُولْسَه	تَمَامِش اُولْسَه	تَمِيَهجَكْ اُولْسَه
تَپَمَسَه	تَپَمَزْ ...	تَپَمَامِش ...	تَپَمِيَهجَكْ ...

Active Participles.
Present.

Aorist.

| تَمِيَهجَكْ اُولُور | تَمَامِش اُولُور | تَمِزْ اُولُور | تَمِزْ |
| تَپَهمَيَهجَكْ ... | تَپَهمَامِش ... | تَپَهمَزْ... | تَپَهمَزْ |

···

Past.

| تَمِيَهجَكْ اُولْمِش | (not used) | تَمِزْ اُولْمِش | تَمَامِش |
| تَپَهمَيَهجَكْ ... | (not used) | تَپَهمَزْ ... | تَپَهمَامِش |

Perfect.

| تَمِيَهجَكْ اُولْدُق | تَمَامِش اُولْدُق | تَمِزْ اُولْدُق | تَمَدِكْ |
| تَپَهمَيَهجَكْ ... | تَپَهمَامِش ... | تَپَهمَزْ... | تَپَهمَدِكْ |

Future.

| (not used) | تَمَامِش اُولَهجَقْ | تَمِزْ اُولَهجَقْ | تَمِيَهجَكْ |
| (not used) | تَپَهمَامِش ... | تَپَهمَزْ ... | تَپَهمَيَهجَكْ |

··

Passive Participles.

Aorist.

| تَمِيَهجَكْ اُولْدُق | تَمَامِش اُولْدُق | تَمِزْ اُولْدُق | تَمَدِكْ |
| تَپَهمَيَهجَكْ ... | تَپَهمَامِش ... | تَپَهمَزْ ... | تَپَهمَدِكْ |

Future.

| (not used) | تَمَامِش اُولَهجَقْ | تَمِزْ اُولَهجَقْ | تَمِيَهجَكْ |
| (not used) | تَپَهمَامِش ... | تَپَهمَزْ ... | تَپَهمَيَهجَكْ |

Verbal Nouns.

Present.

يَهجَكْ اُولْمَه	تَپمامِش اُولْمَه	تَمِز اُولْمَه	تَمامَه
مَيهجَكْ ...	تَپهمامِش...	تَپهمَز...	تَپهمَامَه

Perfect.

يَهجَكْ اُولدُق	تَپمامِش اُولدُق	تَمِز اُولدُق	تَمدِكْ
مَيهجَكْ ...	تَپهمامِش ...	تَپهمَز ...	تَپهمَدِكْ

Future.

(not used)	تَپمامِش اُولَهجَق	تَمِز اُولَهجَق	تَمِيهجَكْ
(not used)	تَپهمامِش ...	تَپهمَز ...	تَپهمِيهجَكْ

Gerunds.

1st.	هجَكْ اُولُوب	تَپمامِش اُولُوب	تَمِز اُولُوب	تَمِيوب
	سيهجَكْ ...	تَپهمامِش ...	تَپهمَز ...	تَپهمِيوب
2nd.	هجَكْ اُولَهرق	تَپمامِش اُولَهرق	تَمِز اُولَهرق	تَمِيدَرك
	سيهجَكْ ...	تَپهمامِش ...	تَپهمَز ...	تَپهمِيدَرك
3rd.	يَهجَكْ اُولِنجَه	تَپمامِش اُولِنجَه	تَمِز اُولِنجَه	تَمِينجَه
	يَهجَكْ ...	تَپهمامِش ...	تَپهمَز ...	تَپهمِينجَه
4th.	يَهجَكْ اُولِيِق	تَپمامِش اُولِيِق	تَمِز اُولِيِق	تَمِيِيِكْ

5th.	تَمِيَه تَمِيَه	تَـمْـزْ اُولَه اُولَه	تَمَامِشْ اُولَه اُولَه	هَجَكْ اُولَه اُولَه
	تَپَمَيَه تَپَمَيَه	تَپَمَزْ ...	تَپَمَامِشْ ...	سَيَهَجَكْ ...
6th.	تَمَامَكِينْ	تَـمْـزْ اُولْمَغِينْ	تَمَامِشْ اُولْمَغِينْ	هَجَكْ اُولْمَغِينْ
	تَپَمَامَكِينْ	تَپَمَزْ ...	تَپَمَامِشْ ...	سَيَهَجَكْ ...
7th.	تَـمِيَهلُو	تَـمْـزْ اُولَهلُو	تَمَامِشْ اُولَهلُو	يَهَجَكْ اُولَهلُو
	تَپَمَيَهلُو	تَپَمَزْ ...	تَپَمَامِشْ ...	يَهَجَكْ ...

Section XVII.

The Dubitative, Potential and Facile Verbs, &c.

The Dubitative Verb is formed by adding the syllable مِشْ (mĭsh, mĭsh), or the word ایمِشْ (ĭmĭsh), to any personal verb, indicative or necessitative, active or passive, affirmative, negative, or impotential; but, in the perfect indicative, it displaces the syllable دِی (dĭ) of the root. It casts a doubt on what is said; and is often added, in conversation, by another speaker, to express that he considers what has been affirmed by the former speaker to be questionable, or hearsay, or mere assumption. When the first speaker uses it himself, he does so to express that what he relates is either doubtful, hearsay, or erroneous assumption, from some other person. It is a gross vulgarism, to which Armenians and European novices are addicted, to use this dubitative syllable, in conversation, where the دى of the perfect indicative, or of any compound tense, is required. In writing, there is no denying that this form is systematically used, by the best authorities, in place of the tense they would employ in speaking. The form has a more musical sound ; and it is, in my opinion, a fruit of imitating Persian verb-forms in Turkish; initiated, probably, by the Persian scribes of the early reigns.

In dubitative conjugation, this syllable مش follows the simple tense-root and its plural, preceding the compound and personal terminations, singular or plural ; unless it be spoken by another person. In this last case, it naturally comes alone, after all other words. Thus : تَـبُورمِشِم (teplyormishim) *it is said, supposed, pretended, suggested, &c., that I am kicking ;* تَـبُورمِش ايدِن (teplyormish idin) *it is said, &c., that thou wast kicking ;* نَرائمِش (teper imish) *it is said, &c., that he kicks ;* تَپِرمِش ايدِك (tepermish idik) *it is said, &c., that we used to kick ;* تَپمِش (tepmish siniz) *it is said, &c., that you kicked or have kicked ;* سدحـكّرائمِش (tepejekler imish) *it is said, &c., that they are going to kick.* (This word or syllable, مش, ایمش, is really the past active participle of the obsolete verb ایمَك.)

The Potential Verb is formed of the fifth gerund (not repeated) followed by the verb بِلمَك (bilmek) in its entire conjugation, the gerund remaining unchanged throughout. This auxiliary verb then means *to be able,* and answers to our

English *can*. Ex.: ‏سه بلمك‎ (tepe bĭlmek) *to be able to kick*; ‏تپه بلیورم‎ (tepe bĭlĭyorĭm) *I am able to kick, I can kick*; &c.

The Facile Verb is formed by the root of a verb, to which an esere is added, followed by a vowel ‏ی‎ and the auxiliary verb ‏ویرمك‎ (vĭrmek, *vulg.* vermek). With a vowel verb other than one in ‏ی‎, a consonantal ‏ی‎, with esere, is added between the root-vowel and the servile ‏ی‎ vowel; and with a verb in vowel ‏ی‎, this is made into a consonant with esere, and the servile vowel ‏ی‎ is then added; as, ‏سویرمك‎ (tepĭ-vĭrmek), ‏قاپلایبویرمك‎ (qaplayĭ-vĭrmek), ‏اوقویویرمك‎ (oqŭyu-vĭrmek), ‏قازیبویرمك‎ (qazĭyĭ-vĭrmek). The sense of these verbs is that of great ease, readiness, off-handedness in the action, which we express in English by saying *just to kick, just to give a kick; just to cover over; just to read* or *recite; just to scratch out*; &c.

• There are several other Turkish verbs in use as special auxiliaries after the gerund of the original verb; as, ‏كلمك‎ (galmek), ‏دورمق‎ (dŭrmaq), ‏قالمق‎ (qalmaq), ‏یاتمق‎ (yatmaq), and ‏یازمق‎ (yazmaq). The first expresses a frequent or natural happening; the next three signify persistency; and the last the idea of having almost happened, of being within an ace of happening. Thus, ‏اوله كلمك‎ (ŏlă galmek) *to happen frequently, of course, as is well known; to be a common occurrence; ‏باقوب دورمق‎ (baqŭp dŭrmaq) *to stand looking; ‏باقه قالمق‎ (baqa qalmaq) *to stand* (remain) *starıng in surprıse and amazement ;*

دوشنـت باتمة. (dushunup yatmaq) *to remaın* (lie) *pondering, in a brown study ;* بالله نازمق (bayîlǎ yazmaq) *to give one's self up* (write) *as about to faint ;* &c., &c., &c.

SECTION XVIII. *The Verb Substantive.*

In Turkish there is no *extant* verb substantive, answering in all its moods and tenses to our verb *to be.* In one sense, the Turkish اولمق performs the office, as an auxiliary and as an independent verb ; but as such, it is a verb adjective, and continually lapses into the parallel idea of *to become.*

The Turkish originally had a true verb substantive, اِمَك (ỉmek) *to be.* This exists fragmentarily in Ottoman Turkish; perhaps in certain persons of the present, certainly in the perfect of the indicative, in the aorist conditional, in the past active participle, in the perfect verbal noun, and in the gerund, apparently modified from the present active participle (which in eastern and old Turkish was and is formed in کان or غان , even قان , traces of which are numerous in Ottoman, as adjectives). Thus :

Indicative.

Present. اِم (ỉm, îm), يِم (yỉm, yîm) *I am ;* سين (sỉn, sîn) *thou art ;* اِز (ỉz, îz), يِز (yỉz, yîz) *we are ;* سكـز (sỉnỉz, sînîz) *you are.*

Perfect. اِدِم (ídím) *I was,* اِدِك (ídín) *thou wast,* اِدِی (ídí)
he was; اِدِك (ídík) *we were;* اِدِکز (ídíníz) *you were;*
اِدِبلَر (ídíler) *they were.*

Conditional Aorist.

اِسَم (ísam) *if I am,* اِسَک (ísan) *if thou art,* اِسَه (íse) *if he is;*
اِسَک (ísek) *if we are,* اِسَکز (ísaníz) *if you are,* اِسَلر
(íseler) *if they are.*

Past Active Participle.

اِمِش (ímísh) *who or which was.*

Verbal Noun Perfect.

اِیدِك (ídík) *the fact of having been.*

Gerund.

اِیکَن (íken, *old* اِیکان íkán) *during the fact of being.*

These fragments are made negative by prefixing the adverb
دِ (díyíl) *not.* Thus, دِیکِم (díyílím) *I am not,*
(díyíl ídím) *I was not;* دِکِل اِسَم (díyíl ísem) *if I am not;*
دِکِل اِدِك (díyíl ídík) *not used as a verbal noun, but replaced*
by اُولمَادِق (ólmadíq) *the negative verbal noun perfect of* اُولمَق;
دِکِل اِیکَن (díyíl íken) *while not being.*

The present tense indicative of the foregoing fragmentary
verb is completed, as to its third persons, singular and plural,

L

by using, when necessary only, the special, unique, and most distinctive Turkish invariable particle of affirmation, ‌دِ (dĭr, dîr) *is*, and its conventional (unnecessary) plural, دِرلَر (dĭrler, dîrlar) *are* (which is just as well expressed by the singular).

This word دِ, written in eastern Turkish دُور (dur), as it is still pronounced in provincial Ottoman, is often found also, in old and eastern writings, under the uncontracted form of دُرُور (durur). This circumstance leads to a suspicion that the word is, originally, the aorist of the ordinary verb دُرمَق (durmaq) *to remain*.

However that may be, the peculiarity of the word is that it is not special to the third person singular, or to the two third persons, singular and plural. It is often used, in writing and in conversation, after a verb of the first or second person also, singular or plural, of any simple tense of the indicative, with or without the plural sign لَر, when the sense admits it. It is, in fact, an exact equivalent to the French inchoative expression *c'est que*, and the Latin *constat quod*, which can be used to introduce any indicative proposition, as the Turkish دِر is used to conclude and complete any such. And, as the French and Latin clauses can be omitted without the sense suffering, so also can the Turkish دِر. In conversation it is much more dispensed with than used.

The negative of دِر is دَكِل دِر (dĭyĭl dĭr) *is not*; pl. دِيكِلّرْدِر

(dĭyĬller dĭr) and دیکل درلر (dĭyĬl dĭrler) *are not* (just as well expressed without the ل).

SECTION XIX. *The Verb of Presence and Absence, of Existence and Non-Existence.*

THERE ARE NO SUCH VERBS IN TURKISH. What there are, and what Europeans have erroneously chosen to designate as such, are two *adjectives*, وَار (var) *present* or *existent*, یوْق (yôq) *absent* or *non-existent*. Like any other substantive or adjective, these may be followed by the verbal particle of affirmation در, which, in this case, as in any other case, may be omitted in conversation.

It may be convenient, occasionally, for a novice in Turkish to suppose that وَار or وَار.دْ means *there is*; that یوْق or یوْق.دْ. means *there is not*. But, unless rightly understood, those renderings are misleading. The expressions really say and mean *he, she, or it, is present* (or *existent*); *he, she, or it, is absent* (or *non-existent*) ; as, آتَش وَار (atesh var) *fire* (is) *present* (here), or *existent* (somewhere); آتش یوق (atesh yôq) *fire* (is) *absent* (here), or *non-existent* (anywhere).

Then, such a phrase as وَار اوْل (var ôl) *be thou present* (or *existent*), یـوق اول (yôq ôl) *be thou absent* (or *non-existent*), becomes clear. The first is a kind of prayer, *Mayest thou ever exist, and be at hand, ready to help the afflicted!* while the

second is a condemnation, a sentence of banishment or
annihilation, or a wish in the nature of a curse, *Away!
Avaunt!* &c.

By using a locative with these two expressions, they become
special instead of general : وار ة,نَار ده. ـ (jeblında pára var)
in my pocket money is present (I have some money in my
pocket) ; أوِبْمَدَه اُوطُونُمْ يُوقْ ادى (evimde odunum yoq idí) *in my
house my firewood was absent, wanting, non-existent* (I had no
firewood in my house).

By using a possessive pronoun (with or without a genitive
as well) with these two expressions, the idea of possession is
superadded ; as, وار نَارەم (param var) *money belonging to me
exists* (i. e., *I have money, I have some money*) ; بوق پا,ەك (paraň
yoq) *money belonging to thee* (is) *non-existent* (i. e., *thou hast no
money*); بابَاسْنك حوق دـَالْرَى وار در (babá-inîn chóq kitablari var
dir) *many books belonging to his father are existent* (i. e., *his
father has many books*); نَـْ سَكَا احْـتَـَاجِمْ يُوقْ ادى (benim sana
ihtiyajim yóq idí) *any need of mine to* (lean on) *thee* (for assist-
ance) *was non-existent* (i. e., *I had no need of thee*).

SECTION XX. *Of the Compound Verbs.*

Besides the Turkish verbs already described, the Ottoman
language has been indefinitely enriched with whole classes of

compound verbs, active and passive, transitive and intransitive, formed by a Turkish auxiliary verb preceded by a substantive or adjective of Arabic or Persian, even of foreign, origin.

An active compound verb is formed, generally, by an Arabic, rarely by a Persian verbal noun, or by a foreign substantive, followed by one of the auxiliaries اِ - ,اِ (ítmek, *vulg.* etmek), أَنْـلَـمَك (eylemek), قَلْمَق (qílmaq) *to do,* or نُورمَق (búyurmaq) *to command, to deign to do;* or by an Arabic (very seldom, a Persian, never a foreign) active participle, followed by the auxiliary أُولمَق (ólmaq) *to be.* These verbs are either transitive or intransitive. The first three auxiliaries are identical in sense; the first is the most frequently used; the second often, the third occasionally, replaces it, so as to avoid repetition; and the fourth is used when a deferential tone is assumed in speaking or writing to or of a superior, and politely to or of an equal. Thus, أَرْسَالْ اِيتْمَك (írsal etmek) *to send;* أَرْسَالْ نُورمَق (írsal buyurmaq) *to deign* or *condescend to send, to favour by sending, to have the goodness to send;* مُوجِبْ أُولمَق (mujíb ólmaq) *to cause;* بُوطِن اَللَمَك (tevattún eylemek) *to settle* (in a place, as a home); نَشِمَان أُولمَق (peshīman olmaq) *to be regretfully or penitently sorry* (for some act); وِيزِيتَـه اِيتْمَك (vízíte etmek) *to visit, to pay a visit.*

Transitive verbs of this class form their passives with the auxiliary أُولنمَق (ólunmaq), which, by itself, does not admit of translation. Thus, اِرْسَال اُوْلُنَمَق (Irsal olunmaq) *to be sent, to have done* (to it) *the action of being sent* (for the Arabic and Persian verbal nouns, the reverse of the more general Turkish rule, take the passive as well as the active sense). Deferential compound passives are formed with the passive auxiliary بُوُرُلمَق (buyurulmaq) ; as, اِرْسَال بِيُورُلمَق (Irsâl buyurulmaq) *to be condescendingly sent, to be kindly sent.*

Reciprocal verbs active of this class are formed with the reciprocal of ايتمك, that is, with the auxiliary ايدِشمَك (Idish-mek) ; as, خصومت ايدِشمَك (khusumet Idishmek) *mutually to exercise hostility, litigation, or spite, towards one another.*

Causatives of the simple and reciprocal are formed by the causatives of ايتمك and ايدِشمَك, namely, ايتدِرمَك, ايدشْدِرمَك ; thus, خصومت ايدِشْدِرمَك *to cause* or *let* (a thing) *be sent* ; اِرْسَال ايتْدِرمَك *to cause* or *let* (two or more) *mutually attack each other.*

Negatives and impotentials, as also dubitatives, potentials, and faciles, are constructed with those forms of ايتمك and the other auxiliaries. Thus, اِرْسَال ايدَهمَامَكْ *not to send* ; اِرْسَال ايتَامَامَكْ *not to be able to send* ; اِرْسَال ايـمـِش *it is said that he sent* ; اِرْسَال ايديويرمك *just to send.* ; اِرْسَال ادَه بِلمَكْ *to be able to send.*

SECTION XXI. *Of the Interrogative Verb, and Interrogation in general.*

All interrogations, in Turkish (when an interrogative pronoun is not present in the phrase, as such), are made by introducing the interrogative particle or adverb می (mĭ, mî) into its proper position in the phrase.

The proper position of this particle in the phrase is the end of the word on which the question turns. We have no equivalent for it in English; in Latin the word *an*, and the enclitic particle *ne*, are its equivalents; also the French *est-ce que?*

This may be best shown by an example of five elements, each of which may be the word on which the question specially turns, so that the adverb مـ is successively joined to each of them to indicate that speciality. Thus:

1. سمی صباح بنمله عربده بنه حکسین (sanmĭ sabah benĭmlâ 'arabâyâ bĭnêjêksĭn)

Is it *thou* who art to ride with me to-morrow in the carriage`

2. سن صباحمی, بمله عربده بنه حکسین (sân sabahmĭ benĭmlâ 'arabâyâ bênêjêksĭn)

Is it *to-morrow* that thou art to ride with me in the carriage?

3. سن صاح بنملهمی عربده بنه حکسین (sân sabah benĭmlamĭ 'arabâyâ bĭnêjêksĭn)

Is it with *me* that thou art to ride in the carriage to-morrow?

4. سَنْ صَبَاحْ بَنْمْلَه عَرَبَيَمِى بِنَهجَكْسِينْ (sån såbāh běmĭmlä 'åråbayå-
mĭ bĭnejěksĭn)

Is it *in the carriage* that thou art to ride with me to-morrow?

5. سَنْ صَبَاحْ بَنْمْلَه عَرَبَيَه بِنَهحَكْمِيسِينْ (san sabah benĭmla 'arabaya
bĭnejěkmĭsĭn)

Art thou *going to ride* with me to-morrow in the carriage?

This does not, however, exhaust the possible points of the question in the case of this sentence, nor the proper places of the adverb مى in it. The phrase itself may be in question, as to whether these words were used, or some others, by the person to whom the interrogation is addressed. In that case, the adverb مى would stand after the personal ending of the verb; سَنْ صَبَاحْ بَنْمْلَه عَرَبَيَه بِنَهحَكْسِينْ مى (san såbah benĭmla 'ara-baya bĭnejeksĭn mĭ), which means, *Dost thou say, thou wilt ride with me to-morrow in the carriage?*

The last two instances call specially for the explanation that, in compound verbs the proper place of the adverb مى may be between the two elements of the verb. Thus we may ask, ارسالْ مى ايدهجَكْ *Is it* to send (and not himself *carry*, for instance) *that he is going to do?* and ارسال ايدهجكمى (ĭrsal ĭdejekmĭ) *Is he going to send?*

In Turkish simple or derivative verbs, supposing that the adverb ، is to follow the verb in the sentence, and not some

other member thereof, then a further question is seen to arise
in No. 5 above given, as to the exact part of the verb itself
that takes this word after it. In this respect, the tenses have
first to be considered. The simple tenses take the adverb at
the end of the tense-root, and their compounds also, before
their auxiliary اٸدی ; thus, اٸدیورمی is he doing? اٸدیورمی اٸدی
was he doing? Next, a distinction has to be made between
the third persons, singular and plural, as one group, and the
first and second persons, singular and plural also, as another
group. The first-named group of tenses have no personal
endings, the second group have special personal endings, and
the interrogative precedes these, following the tense-root still;
thus, تَسٌورمِمْ (teplyŏrmlylm) am I kicking? تِپیورمیمیر (teplyor-
mlsln) art thou kicking? بِپسٌورمی (teplyorml) is he kicking?
تَپیورمِمِز (teplyormlylz) are we kicking? تِپیورمیسکز (teplyŏr-
mlslnlz) are you kicking? تِپیورلَرمی (teplyŏrlerml) are they
kicking?

The perfect tense indicative forms an exception to the foregoing rule, as it takes the interrogative after the personal
endings. Thus, تِپدِمِمی (tepdlmml) have I kicked? did I kick?
تدکمی (tepdlnml) hast thou kicked? didst thou kick? تدیمی
(tepdlml) has he kicked? did he kick? تَپْ دْ . ﻰ (tepdlkml)
have we kicked? did we kick? تدیکزمی (tepdlñlzml) have you
kicked? did you kick? تَدلِرمی (tepdllerml) have they kicked?
did they kick?

SECTION XXII. *Of Adverbial Expressions.*

As explained in Section II., every Turkish adjective is also an adverb.

Every noun of time is also used as an adverb; as, صَبَاح كَل (sabah gâl) *come to-morrow*; ارْكَن كَلْدِى (erken galdî) *he came early*; أَخْشَام كَلِر (akhsham gelir) *he will come in the evening.*

Adjectives of relative place, like all adjectives, are used as adverbs; thus, يُوقَارِى چِيق (yûqarî chîq) *mount up, walk up, climb up, ascend*; اشاغِى كَل (ashâghî gal) *come down, descend*; ايلَرَو كِت (îlerî gît) *go forward, advance*; كَـرُو كَل (gerî gal) *come back.*

But substantives of place, like all substantives, can be used adverbially by the sole means of being joined to prepositions; thus, يُوقَارِيدَه اوتُورِيُور (vuqarîda ôturîyôr) *he is sitting higher up*; أَشَاغِيدَن سِيُورِم (ashaghîdan gelîyorîm) *I am coming from below*; صَاعَه كِت (sagha gît) *go to the right;* &c.

A possessive pronoun may enter into such an adverbial expression; as, أُسْتُمَه حِقْدِى (ustuma chîqdî) *he mounted on to the top of me.*

An adjective, substantive, and preposition may join to form an adverbial expression; as, الت طرفده (alt tarafda) *on the lower side, lower down*; الت طرفدن (ålt taråfdan) *from the lower side; from lower down.*

So an adjective, substantive, possessive, and preposition may be combined in an adverbial expression; as, أُرُسْتُ نَائِمَه (ûst yanîma) *to the side above me;* الت نَائِكَدَه (alt yanînda) *on the side below thee;* صاغ طَرَفِنْدَن (sagh tarafîndan) *from his (her, its) right-hand side.*

With certain special exceptions, any Arabic substantive or adjective becomes an adverb by adding an ustun and vowel ١ to it; this being often marked with a double ustun sign, and read ân; or, if the word is a feminine in ه , by putting two dots, with or without the double ustun sign to it, without an ١; thus, طُولا (tulân) *in length, longwise, in longitude;* عَرْضاً ('arzan) *in breadth, breadthwise, in latitude;* نَرًّا وُ بَحْرًا (berrân ue bahran) *by land and by sea;* مقَدَّما (muqaddema) *formerly;* موخرا mu٭âkhkhâran) *latterly, recently;* قَاطِعاً و قَاطِبَة (qât'an ve qatîbetan) *decidedly and entirely.*

The first ten Arabic ordinals are thus much used adverbially; as, أَوّلاً (âvvâlâ) *firstly;* ثَانِيا (sânîya) *secondly;* ثَالِثا (salîsa) *thirdly;* رَابِعا. (rabî'a) *fourthly;* خَامِسا (khamîsa) *fifthly;* سَادِسا (sadîsa) *sixthly;* سَابِعا (sabî'a) *seventhly;* ثَامِنا (samîne) *eighthly;* تَاسِعا (tasî'a) *ninthly;* عَاشِرا ('âshîra) *tenthly.*

SECTION XXIII. *Of Prepositions.*

They always follow the substantive or pronoun. Besides those given in the chapter on the substantive, there are but four or five others : اوزره (uzere) *upon,* حه (je, ja) *according to,* سز (slz) and سزین (slzln) *without,* لین (leyln) *at the time of, after the manner of.*

SECTION XXIV. *Of Conjunctions.*

The conjunctions ده (da) and دخی (dakhî) *also,* follow the word they unite to a preceding one ; as, كیدرسڭ بن ده كیدرم (gldersan, ben-dâ glderlm) *if thou wilt go, I also will go ;* بو دخی (bu dakhî) *this, too.*

All other conjunctions head the clauses which they connect.

The principal of these are: و (ve, in Persian couplets read u, û) *and* ; اما (amma), لكن (lakln), ولكن (ve-lakln) *but* ; آنجق (anjaq) *only* ; اكر (eyer, eger) *if* ; ناخود (yakhôd) *or* ; یا...یا... (ya... ya...) *either... or...* ; نه... نه... (ne... ne...) *neither... nor...* ; حتّی (hatta) *insomuch that* ; مكر (meyer, meger) *unless* ; امدی (lmdl) *therefore, wherefore* ; زیرا (zıra) *for, because* ; چونكه (chunku) *since, by reason that* ; كه (kl) *that* ; تا (ta) *so that, in order that; as far as.* Of these, some are Turkish, some Arabic, others Persian in origin.

Section XXV. *Of Interjections.*

These are mostly Arabic or Persian in origin. They pre-cede, as in English. The principal are : اي (ey), يا (yā) *O;* آه (ah) *ah;* أَيْوَاه (eywah) *alas;* خَيْف (kháyf) *woe;* مَدَد (meded) *help;* آفَرِين (äferīn, *vulg.* äferĭm) *bravo.*

There is, however, a peculiar Turkish interjection آ (á) *O,* that joins on to the vocative following it ; as, آبَابَا (a-baba) *O father;* آآنَا (a-ana) *O mother.* It also follows nouns, pronouns, and verbs, taking the sense of *Yes! Indeed! I told you so! You see now!* as, أَدَمَا (adam-a) *a man;* you see ! كُوزَلَا (gyuzel-a) *nice; indeed!* بَنِمَا (benĭm-a) *mine; in sooth!* كُورَهمَدَك (gyüremadĭn-a) *thou couldst not see; after all!*

CHAPTER III.

The Ottoman Syntax.

Section I. *Conversational brevity. Precision in writing.*

Colloquial and written Ottoman Turkish, as far as Syntax is concerned, are the very antipodes of each other.

As in the orthography the rule is given : " Never introduce a vowel-letter into a Turkish or foreign word without removing a possible doubt as to pronunciation ; never leave out a vowel in such a word, if by the omission a doubt is created as to pronunciation,"—that is, be always as concise as is possible without falling into ambiguity ; so also, in colloquial syntax the chief rule is : *Never repeat a word, or introduce its equivalent, and never use a subsidiary word, unless for the sake of emphasis;* whereas the golden rule for written language is, *Never omit any word that tends to make a sentence clear and explicit. On the contrary, introduce freely as many new words as may, in the requisite degree, elucidate the sense sought to be conveyed.* In other words, *Spoken Ottoman Turkish should be as concise as possible, even to the verge of ambiguity;*

written Ottoman Turkish must be as full, verbally, as to leave no doubt on the mind of the reader at any distance of space or time.
The reasons are obvious and eminently practical, philosophical; namely: If, by reason of a speaker's conciseness, a doubt as to his meaning should arise in the mind of the person addressed, a question can be put, and the doubt at once removed; if, on the contrary, a written document be left obscure in any part, the doubt thence arising must remain unsolved, and the meaning guessed at, because the writer is either dead or away at a distance.

Hence, if one be asked, بو نه در (bù nè dir) *what is this?* the answer, in Ottoman Turkish, will be, for instance, اَلْمَا (elma) *an apple,* as in English. (A Frenchman would answer: *"C'est une pomme"*) Should the question be, قَرْنْدَاسِمِی کُوْرْدُڭُزمِی (qarndashîmî [*vulg.* qardashîmî] gyurdunuz-mu) *have you seen my brother?* the answer will be, either کُوْرْدُم (gyurdum) *I have seen* (him), or کُوْرمَدِم (gyurmadim) *I have not seen* (him). Should one say to you, بونی سڭا وِرسهم یرمیسڭ (bunù sana versam, yer-mî-sin) *If I give this to thee* (you), *wilt thou* (will you) *eat* (it)? the answer will be either یرِم (yerim) *I will eat* (it), or یَمَم (yemam) *I will not eat* (it). In this last question, the omission of "it," even by the asker, is to be remarked.

As instances of the omission of all possible subsidiary words from phrases in conversation, may be mentioned that of the affirmative دُر (dir) *is, it is, he* or *she is,* on all occasions of ordinary assertion or negation. The personal and corroborative possessive pronouns are never employed in conversation unless for emphasis or distinction ; as, سویورم (savĭyórĭm) *I love* (thee, you, him, her, it), سنی سویورم (sanĭ savĭyorĭm) *I love thee* (you), بن سنی سویورم (ben sanĭ ...) *I, personally, love thee;* باأَم كلدی (babam galdĭ) *my father came,* or *has come.*

As a consequence of the desire to leave no doubt as to the meaning of a writing, nouns and verbs in apposition, in pairs, are much used ; such are, وِدّ و محبّت (vĭdd u mǎhabbet) *friendship,* تحریر و تَسْطِر اولُندی (tǎhrīr u tastīr ólŭndu) *has been written.*

A result of the avoidance of unnecessary repetition is that the third person singular of a verb is often employed instead of its plural when the nominative plural is expressed ; as, آدَمْلَر كَلدی (adamlar galdĭ) *some men,* or *the men have come,* or *came.*

Another such result is the use of a singular substantive with a plural cardinal number ; as, اُوچ اَت (uch at) *three horses,* بِن عَرَبه (bĭn 'araba) *a thousand vehicles* (carriages, carts, waggons, &c.).

To make written composition still more precise, it is very usual, after introducing a common substantive or a proper name into a paragraph or article, letter, dispatch, &c., never to use a personal pronoun to designate the thing or person so named, but to repeat the substantive or proper name as often as may be required, either preceded or followed by one of the indicative adjectives, مَزْبُور (mezbur), مَذْكُور (mezkyur), for things or persons, مَسْفُور (mesfur), for a contemned or criminal person, مُومَى اِلَيْه (muma ïley-h), for a reputable person, and مُشَارُ اِلَيْه (mushārun ïley-h), for a person of rank and consideration. These words all mean, in reality, *the afore-said, the afore-mentioned, the said*, &c. In the case of a *person* first mentioned by name, or by a common substantive, these words may be used as substantives,—we might say,—as a kind of personal or demonstrative pronoun, in all the cases of the declension; but, in the case of a *thing*, they must be used as adjectives to its name, repeated each time.

SECTION II. *Syntax of the Substantive.*

A common noun substantive singular may be either definite or indefinite, and may represent, according to circumstances or the context, either an individual or the individual, several individuals, a portion of the species, or the whole species; as,

بَاغْچَه كُوزَل شَى (båghchå gyûzél shéy) *a garden* (is) *a pretty thing;*

پَادِشَاه كَلْدِى (pādïshāh gåldï) *the monarch came*, or *has come;*

اِنْكِلْتَرَهْ دَه كَمِى جُوق (ïnglïtérådå gémï chôq) *in England* (there are)

many ships : در زِینَتِی باغچَهنِك كَل · (chlchek baghchanîn zînetî dlr) *flowers are the ornaments of the gardens, of the garden ;* صُو ائچدم (sû îchdîm) *I drank* (some) *water, I drank water* (not *wine, &c.*), صُو اقار (sû aqar) *water flows.*

In the accusative case indefinite, the substantive is as in the nominative ; as, صُو ائچمك · اِمٔ (su îchmek) *to drink water* (some water). If the declensional accusative is used, it is always definite ; as, صُو یُو ایچٔدم (sûyû îchdîm) *I drank,* or *have drunk,* the *water.*

There are four different Turkish methods of constructing two substantives in a sentence. First, by simple juxtaposition ; second, by adding the possessive suffix of the third person to the second substantive ; third, by putting the first in the genitive, and still adding the possessive suffix to the second ; and fourth, by putting the first in some other prepositional case, and leaving the second unchanged.

In simple juxtaposition of two substantives, the first indicates a material, the second a form ; or, the first indicates a quantity, the second a material ; as, اَلـتُون قوطِی (altîn qutu) *a gold box ;* بـر كـیـلـه آرْپَـه (bîr kîlê arpa) *a bushel* (of) *barley ;* اِیكَ سَاعَتلِك یُولْ (îkî sa'atlîk yol) *a distance of two hours journey ;* أُوـ سـتـرلِك چوها (ûch setrlîk choha) *broadcloth enough for three coats.*

With the possessive suffix alone added, a relation of genus and species is indicated, the genus standing last, and the combination remaining indefinite; as, كتاب قابى (kitab qabî) *a book-cover*; اوُ كوُپكى (ev kyupeyî) *a house* (domestic) *dog*; یابان اوردکى (yaban urdeyî) *a duck of the wilderness* (wild duck). If the first is a proper name, the second is the species, the first the name of the individual, and the combination is definite; as, آزاق دکزى (azaq denîzî) *the Sea of Azof*.

With the first in the genitive, real possession is indicated, the name of the possessor being the first, and the combination is definite; as, قرالك عسكرى (qîralîn 'askerî) *the king's army*; باباملك اوى (babamîn evî) *my father's house*.

When the first is put into a prepositional case, the second remains without a suffix, and the combination may be definite or indefinite, an active participle being always understood; as, شهره یول (shehrè yôl) *a* (or *the*) *road to the town*; دمیردن كوپرى (demîrdan kyupru) *a bridge of iron*; آنده بر كرّه (aydâ bîr kerre) *once in a month*; &c.

When two substantives are in apposition, no change is made in either; as, چاوش آغا (chawush agha) *Mr. Sergeant*; یازیجى افندى (yazîjî efendî) *Mr. Clerk*; مشیر پاشا (mushîr pasha) *the Pasha* (who is) *a Mushir*. Here, the generic word stands last, and the combination is definite. Sometimes, the specific word or term is complex and obeys its own rules; as, اون باشى اغا (ôn-bashî agha) *Mr. Corporal;* مير الاى بك (mîr-alây bey) *Squire Colonel;* مير لوا پاشا (mîrl-llva pasha) *the Major-General Pasha.*

There are two exceptions to the rule that the generic word stands last, when the other word is a proper name. In all other cases with proper names, this rule holds good; as, اسما سلطان (esma sûltan) *Princess Esma,* عزت مولا (Îzzet môlla) *Judge Izzet;* عارف افندى (arîf êfêndî) *Mr. 'Arif;* &c. The exceptions are: 1, the word سلطان, when applied to the sovereign before his name; as, سلطان عبد الحميد (sûltan 'abdu-'l-hamîd); 2, the word مولا, when applied to a student or schoolboy, also before his name; as, مولا راشد (molla rashîd) *schoolboy Rashid.*

Any number of substantives may be in apposition, and one of them may be the proper name of the individual; as, اوغلم قولكز (ôghlum qûlunûz) *your servant, my son;* اوغلم رفیق بك قولكز (ôghlûm refîq bey qulunuz) *your servant, my son, Refiq Bey;* اوغلم مير الاى رفیق بك قولكز (oghlûm mîr-âlay refîq bey qulunuz) *your servant, my son, Colonel Refiq Bey;* &c.

When a string of substantives in construction would in strictness require several of them consecutively to be put in the genitive case, the monotonous cacophony of the repetition of the preposition is avoided by omitting it once or twice where most appropriate; thus, اتی اوغْلُنِك دایِیسِنِك استه سِنِك باشانِك (pashanîn enîshtesînîn dayîsînîn oghlunuñ atî) *the horse of the son of the uncle of the brother-in-law of the pasha*, may be expressed in either of the following ways : باشانِك اَنشْتَهسی دار یِسی

باشا اَنشْتَهسی or , باشا اَنْشْتَهسِنِك دایِسی اُوعْلنِك آتی or , اُوعْلِنِك آنِی

the last ; باشانِك اَنشْتَهسی دار ....نِك اُوعْلنِك آتی or , دابِسِنِك اُوعْلنِك آنِی genitive preposition being, perhaps, the most frequently retained and necessary.

Two or more Arabic or Persian substantives may be put in Persian construction with each other. Their order is then the reverse of what it would be in Turkish construction, just as in English *the king's horse* is in reverse order with *the horse of the king.* In Persian construction each preceding substantive of a series must be *vocally* connected with its consequent. This *vocal connexion* is effected by making the final quiescent consonant of the preceding substantive movent with eseré; thus, فَرْمَان شَاه (fermanî shah) *the command of the king;* مضمون ورمَانِ شَاه ابران (muzmunu fermanî shahî îran) *the tenour of the command of the king of Persia.* But, if the last consonant of a preceding substantive is movent, and followed by a vowel-letter, a servile consonant must be introduced to support the eseré vowel of connexion; and this consonant varies

with the final vowel of the word. When the final vowel-letter
is ا or و, the servile consonant is ى; as, حاى نـاى أَسْـب (ja-yi
pa-yi esb) *the place of the foot of the horse;* مُوى رُوى سَكْ (mu-
yu ru-yu seg) *the hair of the face of the dog.* If the final
vowel-letter be a ى, this letter is converted itself into the
servile consonant required; so that no written addition is
needed; thus, پَرِي حاه بُرْ ـ (pèri-yi chah-i burj) *the fairy of the
well of the tower.* Ignorance often writes a hemze over such
final ى so converted into a consonant; but it really is not
requisite. If, however, the final vowel be the letter ه, then
the addition of a hemzè is a necessity. Sometimes the esere
vowel-sign is figured under it, ﺋ. Usage is divided as to the
proper place where the servile hemzè should be written. It
is at times more correctly placed between the two words, on a
line with the writing; as, بَرَهء فَلَكْ (bere-i felek) *the lamb of
the sphere* (i.e., *Aries*); and otherwise it is less correctly placed
over the vowel ه; as, بَرَهء فَلَكْ.

Of two substantives in Persian construction, the first is often
the metaphorical name of the thing literally expressed by the
second, the pair really representing one idea under two images;
as, سائـق تـقـدر (sa'iqi taqdīr) *the drover, destiny;* عنَان عزِيمت
('inani 'azimet) *the reins* (of) *departure.*

Whether in Turkish or Persian construction, the same
remark holds good of a pair of substantives, one of which is

the word اَمْر (emr), or one of its synonyms, مَادَّه (madde), خُصُوص (khusus), كَيْفِيَّت (keyfîyyet), &c., all of which signify our *circumstance,* and the like. They are used in written Turkish for precision. Thus: راه تَحْصِيلِك اَمْر انْسِلاكِى (rah-î tah-sîlîn emr-î însîlakî) *the matter of the pursuit of the path of study ;* دُونَانْمَهْنِك كَلْمَسِى خُصُوصِى (donanmanîn gelmesî khûsusu) *the question of the coming of the fleet.*

After a proper name of a person or thing, the word نَام (nam) *name,* is commonly employed ; as, اَحْمَد نَامْ ذَاتْ (ahmed nam zat) *the personage named Ahmed ;* قِرِمْ نَامْ حَزِيره (qîrim nam jezîre) *the island (peninsula) named Crimea.*

The two words حَضْرَتْ (hazret), جَنَابْ (jenāb), which originally mean *presence* and *side,* are used before or after the names or titles of individuals held in honour, with a meaning varying from that of *His Divine Majesty* down to that of plain *Mr.* or *Mrs.,* &c. When they precede, they remain unchanged to the eye, but are in Persian construction ; as, حَضْرَتِ خُدَا (hazret-î khudā) *His Divine Majesty, God ;* حَضْرَتِ پَيْغَمْبَر (-- peygâmber) *His Sanctity, the Prophet ;* جَنَابِ پَادِشَاهْ (jenab-î padîshah) *His Majesty, the Sovereign ;* جَنَابِ صَدَارَتْمَآبْ (— sadaret-maʾab) *His Highness, the Repair of the Vezirate* (the Grand Vezir). When they follow, they are in Turkish construction, and generally take the possessive pronominal

suffix of the third person plural, but sometimes that of the
third person singular ; as, شیخ الاسلام طاهر بك حصرتلری، (sheykhu-
'l-Islam tahir bey hazretleri) *His Eminence the Lord High
Chancellor, Tahir Bey* ; بروسه مفتیسی حَسَنْ افَنْدی جناسی (burusa
muftisi hasàn efendi jenabi) *His Honour the State Counsel of
Brusa, Hasan Efendi* ; سفیرْ باشا حضرتلری (sefir pasha —) *His
Excellency the Pasha Ambassador*; ترجمَان بك جَنَانلَری (terjuman
bey —) *His Worship the Interpreter Bey*; &c., &c., &c.
Generally, the word حضرت before a single name indicates one
of the prophets, saints, or patriarchs of old ; as, حضرت نوح
(hazreti nūh) *the patriarch Noah* ; مُوسَی - (— musa) *the
prophet Moses* ; سلمان — (— suleymān) *the prophet* (king)
Solomon ; مَرْیَم — (— meryem) *Saint Mary* (the Virgin
Mother); عیسی — (— isa) *the Prophet Jesus* ; مَسیح —
(— mesih) *the holy Anointed One* (Christ); &c., &c., &c.

Section III. *Syntax of the Adjective.*

Nearly everything requisite in a sketch has been said on
this subject in the former Chapter (II.), Section II. If several
adjectives qualify one substantive, they follow one another
simply in Turkish construction, and are all connected vocally
in the Persian construction ; as, کوزَل ادبلو مَحجوبْ جوحَه (gyūzèl,

edebll, mahjub chojuq) a *pretty, well-behaved, modest child;*

فَـزَا فَرَحْ نِمَاي هِشْت ، حَاي (jā-yı̇ blhı̇sht-numa-yı̇ ferah-feza) a *paradise-like, joy-giving place.*

One adjective may qualify several substantives in a sentence; as, سائرہ واحسال و امـ (umem u ejyali sa)lre) *the other peoples and nations.*

An Arabic or Persian adjective is never placed *after* a Turkish or foreign substantive; and whenever either is placed *before* one of these, it remains, like a Turkish adjective, unchanged as to gender or number; as, طاغ عظم ('azım dagh) a *great mountain;* بادشاه عظـ ('âzīm padlshah) a *great monarch,* دوَلْت عظـمْ ('azīm devlet) a *great state.*

Some adjectives take a substantive as a complement to restrict their application. In Turkish construction, this complement precedes, with or without a preposition; as, طولو صو (sù dolù) *full (of) water,* طولو ايله صو (su llâ dolù) *filled with water.* In Persian construction it follows; as, بِيَان لائق (layîq-ı̇ beyan) *worthy of exposition;* طبع موافـق (muwaflq-ı̇ tâb') *conformable with nature.*

The Turkish adjective كِبِى (glbı̇) *like,* follows substantives, the personal pronoun of the 3rd pers. plur., the demonstratives plural, the interrogatives singular and plural, and the compound relatives, when its complements, without any change occurring in them; as, كبى صوو (su glbı̇) *like water;* انلرکـ (anler

gİbİ) *like them;* بُونْلَرْكِبِی (bunlar gİbİ) *like these;* كَـ'ـكِبِی
(kİm gİbİ) *like whom?* نَلَرْكِی (neler gİbİ) *like what things?*
بَابَامِكِی بِـی (babamİnkİ gİbİ) *like the one belonging to my*
father; بنْدهكِی كِـی (bendekİ gİbİ) *like the one I have.* All
other pronouns are put in the genitive, when complements to
this word; as, سـ كِبِی (benİm gİbİ) *like me;* انك كبی (anİī
gİbİ) *like him, her, it;* سِزْك كِی (sİzİn gİbİ) *like you;* بِونِنك كِی
(bunun gİbİ) *like this;* &c.

SECTION IV. *Syntax of the Numerals.*

The Turkish and Persian cardinals always precede their
substantive, and this is usually left in the singular, whatever
the number; as, ايكِی حفت. (İkİ chİft) *two pairs;* دو جهَان (du
jİhān) *the two worlds* (present and future). But the Arabic
cardinal follows, the construction is made Persian, and the
substantive is made plural; as, قوَای خمـَه (qȗvayİ khamse) *the*
five senses; حهات ستته (jİhatİ sİtte) *the six directions* (in space),
six sides (of a solid).

The Turkish and Persian numerals precede the adjectives of
the same substantive; as do also the Arabic (though after the
substantive); thus, ايكِی ساه لحِی (İkİ sİyah kechİ) *two black*
goats; هفت اقلِـم معمورة (heft İqlİm-İ ma'mure) *the seven climates*

of the habitable earth; فواى خَمْسَهءِ اَه (qùvayî khamse-i zā-hìre) *the five external senses.*

But if, instead of an adjective, a descriptive phrase should qualify the substantive, the Turkish numeral comes between the two; as, اوطهبك بويندة برايپ (odanìn bòyunda bìr ìp) *a string of the length of the room;* هَرّبرى بَشْ كَيْسَه آقْچَه ادَرْ بَدَى اَلْمَاسْ (her bìrì besh keysè aqcha eder yedì elmâs) *seven diamonds, each of the value of five purses of money.*

A Turkish cardinal number can be placed after a substantive in the genitive, singular or plural. It does not then define the number of that substantive, but of a definite portion of what this represents; as, آدمك برى (adamìn bìrì) *one of mankind, a man;* آدَمْلَرِكْ برى (adamlerìñ bìrì) *one of the men;* اُوطَهزِك ايكِيسى (odanìn ìkìsì) *two rooms,* اُوطَهلَرِكْ ايكِيسى (odalarìn ìkìsì) *two of the rooms.*

Very often, between the Turkish cardinal number and its substantive, another substantive is introduced, with the sense of *individual* or *individuals,* as in our phrases "*ten head of cattle,*" "*six sail of ships,*" &c. This substantive varies in Turkish according to the nature of the things defined by the numeral. For *men* it is نفر (nefer) *individual;* for *beasts* it is رَأْس (re's) *head;* for *bulbs* it is بَاشْ (bash) *head;* for *ships* it is قَطعه (qìt'a) *piece;* for *cannons, ships,* and *villages,* it is بَارهْ (pare,

vulg. parȧ) *piece;* for things *usually counted* it is عَدَدْ ('ȧded)
number; for things *not usually counted* it is دانه (dȧne, *vulg.*
tana) *berry;* for *swords* it is قَـبْـضَه (qabza) *hilt;* for *elephants,*
زَنْجِیر (zȧnjīr) *chain.* Thus : بَشْ نَفَرْ آدَمْ *five men;* اون رَأْسْ قُویُونْ
ten sheep; اِیکِی بَاشْ صُوغَانْ *two onions;* یِکِرْمِی قِطْعَه سَفِینَه *twenty
ships;* د سُـرمِی رُه بَه نَـه *twenty vessels;* اون نَاره طُوبْ *ten cannon*
(pieces of artillery); اَللِی پَاره کُوی *fifty villages;* یُوزْ عَدَدْ یُـومُورْطَه
a hundred eggs; اِیکِی دانه اِنْجُو *two pearls;* اُوچْ قَبْضَه قِـلِـجْ *three
swords;* بِـرْ زَنْجِیر فِـلْ *one elephant.*

The Turkish ordinals precede their substantives; as, بِرِنْجِی کِیجَه
(bȧrȧnjȧ geyje) *the first night;* آلْـتْـمِـشْ دُقُـوزْ الای (ȧltmȧsh
dȯqȗzȗnju ālay) *the sixty-ninth regiment.*

The Arabic ordinals follow; as, بَاب خَامِس (bābȧ khāmȧs)
chapter the fifth.

The Persian ordinals generally precede, but sometimes
follow.

The Turkish distributive numerals are used to express the
rates of collection as well as of distribution; as, بَشَرْ پَاره وِیرْدِیلَرْ
(besher parȧ verdȧler) *they contributed five paras each;* اَنْلَره بِشَرْ
نَاره وِیـرِلْدِی (anlarȧ besher parȧ verȧldȧ) *to them five paras each
were distributed.*

For emphasis sake, the simpler distributives are often

repeated; but they are then generally used as substantives; as,

بِرَرْ بِرَرْ طُوپْلَادِمْ (bìrer bìrer tòpladîm) *I collected* (them) *one by one;*

اِیکِ شَرْ اِیکِیشَرْ آلِیکِزْ (ìkìsher ìkìsher alînîz) *take ye* (them) *two apiece each* (of you), *or, take you* (or thou, them) *two together each time.*

SECTION V. *Syntax of Pronouns.*

The demonstrative pronoun, when an adjective, precedes all other qualifications of its substantive; as, بُو اُوچ بِیُوكْ كُوزَلْ كَلِینْلِكْ قِیزْ (bù uch bìyuk gyuzel gellulìk qîz) *these three tall, handsome, nubile girls.*

The suffixed possessive pronoun is not, in literary style, necessarily attached to its substantive, but to the last word of the combination of substantive, adjective, &c., to which it belongs. Thus, مَرْحُومْ پَدَرِمْ (merhum pederìm) *my late father,* may be rendered in the Persian form, پَدَرِ مَرحُومِمْ (peder-ì merhumum); so also, وَحِ خَاطِرخُواهِمِزْ (vejh-ì khatîr-kh'āhìmîz) *the manner desiderated in mind by us* (i. e., *by me*); اقطارِ شرقِیه سرعسکرِ ظَفَرْرَهْبَرِی (aqtar-ì sharqîyye ser-'asker-ì zafer-rehberî) *the victorious commander-in-chief of the eastern districts;* بُو بَاغِنْ هَرْ بِرْ جَای جَانْ فَزَای بِهِشْتِ اِنْتِمَاسِی (bu bàghìn her bìr ja-yî jan-feza-yî bìhìsht-ìntìmāsì) *each soul-enrapturing, paradise-prognosticating spot of this garden.*

The corroborative of the suffixed possessive pronoun of

Turkish construction precedes the whole combination to which the possessive is suffixed ; and this corroborative is always in the genitive, whether it be a substantive or a pronoun ; as, نِــمْ مَرْحُومْ يَــدِرِمْ (benîm merhum pederîm) *my late father* ; أُوطَهنِكْ بِـيُوكْ قَپُوسِى (odanîn bîyuk qapûsu) *the great door. of the room.*

One possessive suffix may qualify several substantives ; as, ال و اَصْحَاب و عِترت و احْمَابِى (al û as-hāb û 'îtret û ahbabî) *his family, companions, posterity, and friends.*

SECTION VI. *Syntax of the Verb.*

Verbs of the first and second person agree with their nomi-natives in number and person ; as, بن دُوردِم (ben gyurdum) *I saw, have seen* (him, her, it, &c.) ; سز دُوردِـكَـز (sîz gyurdunuz) *you saw, have seen* (me, us, them, &c.).

A verb of the third person must also agree with its subject, if *understood ;* as, كُوردِى (gyurdu) *he, she, it saw, has seen* (it,&c.); كُوردِلَر (gyurduler) *they saw, have seen* (it, &c.).

When the subject is *expressed* of a verb of the third person, the verb does not always agree with it in number. A singular subject sometimes has its verb in the plural, out of respect or politeness ; a plural subject often has its verb in the singular, so as to avoid the cacophony of repetition.   Thus : بَابَمْ كَـتْدِيلَر

(bâbâm gitdiler) *my father went, has gone, is gone* ; اوشاقلری کَلدی
(ushaqleri galdi) *his* or *their servants came*, or *have come*, *are
come.*

So a verb with several subjects expressed, when all of the
third person, singular or plural, may be in the singular ; as,
الوف رِضْوان و صُنُوفِ عِفْرَان شَاَیَان دِرْ (uluf-i rizvan ú sunuf-i gufrān
shayan dir) *thousands of prayers for God's acceptance, and all
kinds of wishes for God's mercy* (on him, &c.) *is* (are) *fitting.*

If one of them be of the second person, singular or plural,
and the other or others of the third person, the verb must be
of the second person plural ; as, سَنْ وَ بَدَرِمْ وَ قُوکْشُکْزْ بَرَابَرْ کَتْدِکَزْ
(san ve pederim ve qônshunûz bêraber gitdiniz) *thou and my
father, with your neighbour, went together.*

And if one be of the first person, even singular, whether the
others be of the second or third, singular or plural, the verb
must be in the first person plural ; as, بَنْ وَ سَنْ وَ قَرِنْدَاشِكْ کُوْرْدُكْ
(ben, ve san, ve qarndashin, gyurduk) *I, and thou, and thy
brother, saw* (him, &c.).

In conversation, دِرْ and its plural دِرْلَرْ are generally omitted
at the end of a phrase, affirmative, negative, or interrogative ;
as, کَیْفِکْزْ ایومی (keyfiniz iyi mi) *is your health good ?* ایو (iyi)
it is good ; ایو دکل (iyi diyil) *it is not good.*

But, in repeating the affirmative or negative words of
another, دِرْ must be introduced ; as, بُویْلَه دِرْ دَیُو تَصْدِیقْ اَیْلَدی

(buyle dîr, deyu, tâsdîq eyledî) *he confirmed, saying, " It
is so."*

In relating the words of another, no alteration is permitted
in number, person, or tense of the verb; as, كلورم ددى (gelîrîm,
dîdî) *he said, "I will come"* (not as in English, *"he said he
would come"*).

When the object of a transitive verb is definite, it is put in
the accusative; as, آتی آلدَم (atî aldîm) *I bought, have bought* (or
taken) the horse. But, if the object be indefinite, it remains in
the nominative; as, ات آلدم (at aldun) *I bought a horse* or
horses.

Intransitive, like transitive, verbs, govern their indirect
objects by means of different prepositions, *i.e.*, the substantives
or pronouns are put into different cases according to the verb.
Thus : اولومدن قورقمق (ûlumdan qorqmaq) *to be afraid* of *death ;*
اولومدن قاچمق (ulumdun qachmaq) *to run away* from *death ;*
پاره‌ه باقمق (paraya baqmaq) *to look* at *money* (*i.e.*, to take money
into account or consideration); صوده يوزمك (suda yuzmek) *to
swim* in *the water;* دكزه كيرمك (denîzè gırmek) *to go* into
the sea (*i.e.*, to bathe in the sea); قلج ايله اورمق و لـ (qîlîj îla wur-
maq) *to strike* with a (or *the) sword ;* خاطر ايچون ياپمق (khatîr
îchîn yapmaq) *to do* (a thing) out of *regard* (for some one);
حيانه بنمك (haywanâ bînmek) *to mount* on a *beast* (horse);

كَـمِـىيَه بِنْمَكْ (gemĭye bĭnmek) *to mount* (go) on board *ship*;

آيَاغَه قَـالْقَمَقْ (ayagha qalqmaq) *to rise to one's feet* (*i. e.*, to rise,

get up, stand up).

Nouns of time and place are often used adverbially (as also is the case in English) without prepositions after verbs; as, نَارِين كَل (yarĭn gal) *come to-morrow*; اَشَاعِ اين (ǎshaghĭ ĭn, *vulg.* en) *descend, come* or *go down*; يوقَارِى حَق (yuqarĭ chĭq) *ascend, mount*; i. e., *come* or *go up.* Still, on occasions, prepositions are used with them; as, صَاعَه صَاتْ (saghǎ sap) *deviate* (turn) *to the right*; صُولَه بَاقْ (sŏla bǎq) *look to the left*; كَـرُو كَتْ (gĭrŭ, *vulg.* gerĭ gĭt) *go back*; كَـيْرُودَنْ كَلْ (gerĭdan gal) *come from the rear, from behind.*

A transitive verb has sometimes two direct objects, one definite, the other indefinite; as, اَنِى مُشِـرْ اَتْدِلَرْ (anĭ mushır etdĭler) *they made him a* mushır (duke, or field-marshal).

An Ottoman compound verb, active or passive, often takes its direct or indirect object into the body of the verb, as the Persian complement of its nominal factor; as, نُو دَبِقَدَه تَحْصِيل وُوقُفْ اَنْلَدِى (bŭ daqīqaya tahsılĭ vwuquf eyledĭ) *he acquired cognizance of* (about) *this subtle point*; صَرْفْ مُزْجَات بِضَاعَه قِلِنْدِى (sarf-ĭ muzjat-ĭ bĭza'a qĭlĭndĭ) *expenditure of the modicum of capital was made* (i. e., the *modicum* of capital was spent).

SECTION VII. *Syntax of the Participle.*

In conversation, the substantive qualified by a particle, active or passive, is sometimes understood, and the participle is used as a substantive; as, گلنه وير (gelané ver) *give* (thou it) *to him* (or *her*) *who comes* ; باقمه ـسدیکمه (gidiyimá baqma) *look not at that which I wear* ; یاپه حغمی صورمه (yapajaghimi sorma) *ask not what I shall do.*

The active participle present of اولمق, i. e. اولان, is often omitted after Arabic participles, active or passive ; as, ربع مسکونده واقع ممالك وبلدان (rûb'i méskyûndá vwáqi' mémálik ú bûldan) *the countries and towns situated in the inhabited quarter* (of the globe); نو کتابده مذکور فنون ومعارف (bu kitabda mez-kyur fûnun ú ma'arif) *the sciences and matters of knowledge mentioned in this book.*

Active participles govern all their objects in the same way as the verbs from which they derive ; so also do the passive participles, excepting only the object they each qualify as an adjective; as, قپو آحان (qapú achan) *he who opens a door;* قپویو آحان (qápúyú achan) *he who (that which) opens the door;* اَلـم ایله آحدنغم قو (elim ilé achdighim qapú) *the door that I opened with my hand;* پدریك بونی قول ادهمیهجكی سبب (pederi-min bunú qabul idemeyejeyi sebeb) *the reason for which my father will not be able to accept this.*

The Persian and Arabic participles are constructed, generally, with their objects, in the same manner as if the
participles were substantives ; as, خَالِق هَرْ دُو جِهَان (khaliq-î her
du jihan), هـ دد هجهانك خَالِقِي (her du jihanîn khaliqî) *the Creator
of both worlds;* مخْـلُوق يِـد قـدرتِى (makhluq-u yed-î qudretî),
يِـد قدرتلَرِنك مخلوقى (yed-î qudretlerînîn makhluqu) *the creature
of the hand of His almighty power;* اورننده‌ء اين و ان (aferinende-
î in û an) *the Creator of this and that (all things);* رسـده‌ء كَنـكُره‌ء
حرب أثِير (reside‌î kyungyure-‌î charkh-î esîr) *which has reached
the battlement of the ethereal sphere.*

But sometimes Arabic active participles of transitive verbs
govern their direct objects as do their verbs ; thus, كَـه‌ـ هـ ج
مذّكُوره‌يى مَـسـين (keyfîyyet-î mezkyure-î mubîn) *which explains
the said circumstance.*

SECTION VIII. *Syntax of the Verbal Nouns and Infinitive.*

Turkish verbal nouns are constructed with their subjects,
when substantives, as any two substantives ; thus, أحَـمَدك كَـلمَسى
(ahmedîn galmesî) *the coming of Ahmed, Ahmed's coming;*
احمدك مدیگ (ahmedîn galdîyî) *Ahmed's (past action of) having
come;* احمدك كَلَه‌حكى (ahmedîn gelejeyî) *Ahmed's (future action
of) coming.*

When the subject is a pronoun, it is put in the genitive still, and the Turkish verbal noun takes the possessive suffix of the subject's number and person; as, بنم كلمم (benim galmem) *my coming*; سنك كلدیكك (sanin galdiyin) *thy having come*; كلهجكلرى (aulerin galejekleri) *their future coming*.

Turkish verbal nouns and infinitives are constructed with their objects, direct or indirect, exactly as their verbs; thus, أنى كورمهم ازمیره (ani gyurmem) *my seeing him (her, it)*; كلهجكك (izmiré galejeyin) *thy future coming to Smyrna*· بدرینه أحمدك دون مكتوب یازدیغی، (pederina ahmedin dun mektub yazdighi) *Ahmed's having written a letter to his father yesterday*.

Arabic verbal nouns are constructed with their agents sometimes in the Turkish, sometimes in the Arabic, and sometimes in the Persian manner; as, ورودم (vurudüm) *my arrival*; تحصیلك (tahsilin) *thy study*; تحریری (tahriri) *his writing*; صنع الله suu'a 'llah), صنع الله (sun-i llah) *the act of God*; اداره درکار أفکار (idare-i pergyar-i efkyar) *a revolving of the compasses of the thoughts*.

Arabic verbal nouns are constructed with their objects in the same manner as the compound verbs formed of them; as, مقدوری صرف قن (maqduri sarf) *an employing one's utmost*; جغرافیایی تحصیله مدار (fann-i jagrafiyayi tahsila medar) *a help to an acquiring the science of geography*. But they may also be constructed with them as two simple substantives, either in

the Turkish or Persian manner; as, صَرْفِ مَقْدُورَكْ or مَقْدُورُ صَرْفِ;
and again, حَصْلَنَه جَغْرَافَانَكْ or جَغْرَافَانَه فَنِّ or فَنّ تَحْصِل; &c.

In all cases excepting their construction with their subjects or objects, the Turkish verbal nouns and infinitives are constructed in sentences exactly like any other substantives; as, أُولَمَكْ بُونْدَنْ اَوْلَى دُرْ (ûlmek bûndan evla dîr) *to die is better than this*; قُورْتُلْمَغَه جَالِشْدَى (qurtûlmagha chalîshdî) *he laboured at escaping* · ناقَمَق اِيجُونْ تَرْتِب اتْدِم (yâqmaq îchîn tertîb etdîm) *I arranged, have arranged* (it) *for burning*; كَلْمَسِى لَازِمْ دَكِلْ (gâl-mesî lâzîm dîyîl) *his coming* (is) *not necessary*; كِيدَه بِيلَه جَكِمَه شُبْهَمْ وَارْ (gîde-bîlejeyîme shub-hem var) *my doubt exists*, i. e., *I have a doubt as to my being able to go.*

SECTION IX. *Syntax of the Gerunds.*

The gerunds are not much used in conversation; there the discourse is broken up into as many sentences as may be needed, each with its personal verb; as, كَتْدِم بُوردِم كَلْدِم خَبِر وِيردِم (gîtdîm, gyûrdûm, galdîm, khâber verdîm) *I went; I saw; I came; I gave information.*

But, in the literary style, one long phrase, ending with one personal verb, will contain a number of clauses, each ending with a gerund (which thus acts to the ear, as well as to the eye, like our commas and semicolons); as, دِيدُوب بُورِهرَكْ كَلدَكْدَه

خَر وبردِم (gĭdâp, gyûrerck, galdĭkde, khaber verdĭm), *I, going and seeing, on coming back, reported.*

When compound verbs are used, the auxiliary gerunds may be omitted once or twice in a long sentence ; as, بر موضعه ورود وَ اَنْدَه بِرْ مِقْدَارْ قُعُودْ اِيدُوبْ (bĭr mĕvzĭ'â vûrūd, vĕ ândâ bĭr mĭqdār qû'ūd edup, ...) ... *arriving at a certain place, and sitting down there awhile*, ... In this case, however, a conjunction requires to be introduced in lieu of the gerund omitted ; as is seen in the example given.

The subjects, and direct or indirect objects, of the gerunds are constructed as with their verbs. But, as the gerunds cannot indicate the person and number of their subjects, the appropriate personal pronoun must be expressed before them, when the subject is not a substantive ; as, آدَمْ دَ : اتْ اُوقُوبُوبْ (adam kĭtab ôqûyûb) *man, reading a book* (or *books*), ... ; فَرْمَانِمْ سِزَه وَاصِلْ اُولِيجَیْ (fermanĭm sĭze vwāsĭl olĭjaq) *at what time my command shall attain unto you*, ...; بن شُو آدَمِ كُورَهرَك (ben, shu adamĭ gyurerek) *I, seeing that man*, ... ; &c.

Section X.   *Syntax of the Adverb.*

The adverb precedes the verb or adjective qualified by it ; as, صباحلین كلدی (sâbahleyĭn galdĭ) *he came in the morning* ; چوق كوزَلْ (chôq gyúzél) *very pretty.*

The negative لا (díyíl) *not*, precedes the verb substantive, expressed or understood, but follows the substantive or adjective which it negatives; as, كَنِج دكَ.لا (genj díyílím) *I am not young;* عقلسز دكسين (áqlsíz díyílsín) *thou art not unintelligent;* آدَم دكل در (adám díyíl dír) *he or it is not a man;* &c.

The adverbial suffixes دك (dek), دكين (déyín), follow a noun of time, place, or condition, in the dative; as, صَاحه دكين (sabaha deyín) *until morning;* لوندرهيهدك (londurayadek) *as far as London;* اولومهدك (úlumedek) *until death.* They follow the third gerund also, put in this same dative case, and thus form a verbal limit of time; as, كلينجهيهدك (gelínjeyedek) *until* (I, thou, &c.) *come, came.* The agent must be named or understood; as, بن ديدنجهمهدك (ben gídínjeyedek) *until I go* (or *went*); مَكتوبم اورايه وارنجهمهدك (mektubúm óraya varínjayadek) *until my letter reach* (or *reached*) *there.* The tense of this gerund is decided by the context, in like manner as its agent and object.

The adverb كُوره (gyúre) *according*, also follows a dative; as, عقلمه كُوره ('aqlíma gyure) *according to my judgment;* كَنه كُوره (baná gyure) *according to me;* &c.

The adverbs يَكَ (yana), طولايي (dólayí), اوتورى (úturu) *relatively*, follow substantives or infinitives in the ablative; as, كتابدَن طولايي (kítabdan dólayí) *relatively to* (about) *a* (or *the*) *book ;* كِتْمَكْدَ دْ اُوْنُور (gĭtmekdan uturu) *relatively to* (abont, concerning) *going.*

Although it is not grammatically erroneous, in answering a question, to use the affirmative adverb اوت (evet) or بلي (bell) *yes,* or the negative يوق (yoq) or خَيْر (khayr) *no,* when appropriate, it is unidiomatic to do so. The more general custom, whether one of those adverbs be used or not, is to repeat the word or words of the question on which the interrogation turns, with such grammatical modifications as may be necessary. Thus, turning back to the five questions instanced in Chap. II., sect. 21 (p. 151-2), the respective answers may be : 1, اوت بن (evet, ben) *yes, I* (am to ride); 2, يوق اولِرِكون (yoq, ŏlbĭr gyun) *no, the day after ;* &c.

SECTION XI. *Syntax of the Preposition.*

The Turkish preposition always follows the word it governs, noun, pronoun, or verbal derivative, as is seen in Chap. II., sections 1 (p. 51), 4 (p. 82), 5 (p. 88), 6 (p. 89), 7 (p. 90), and in Chap. III., section 8 (p. 179) ; but the Arabic and Persian prepositions always precede ; as, علي التَّحقِيق ('ale 't-tahqĭq) *in truth ;* برْ قرا (ber qarar) *in permanence* (without change); علي حِدَّه ('ala hĭde) *singly ;* فى الْوَاقِع (fĭ 'l-wäqĭ') *in fact ;* بأىّ حَال (bĭ-eyyĭ halln) *in any case ;* علَى كَلَا التَّقْدِيرِن ('ala kélà 't-taqdiıeyn) *upon either supposition;* از سر نو (ez ser-ì nèv) *from a new beginning* (over again, again).

A preposition may govern two or more substantives in a sentence; as, اَلٌ وَاَصْحَابُ وعِتْرَتُ واَحْبَابَه *to his family, companions, posterity, and friends.*

But, as the Arabic and Persian preposition precedes the adjectives that qualify, as well as the substantives qualified, so the Turkish preposition is placed after all these; consequently, in Persian construction, and when the substantive is followed by the possessive suffixes, the Turkish preposition is separated from the substantive it governs, sometimes by a considerable distance; as, نَادَا ابلَه (baba-m ìle) *with my father;* بُو مُحِبٌّ صَادِقْدَه (bù muhìbb-ì sadìq-dà) *in this faithful friend;* قَالِيُونْ، دره نُون هُمَايُونُكْ بَاشِى (qallyun-ì kyub-numun-ì hùmayunun bashì) *the head of the mountain-like imperial galley.*

SECTION XII. *Syntax of the Conjunction.*

All conjunctions, except the enclitic دٔ (de, da), or دخِى (dàkhì), *too, also,* head the phrase they belong to.

The enclitic conversational دٔ, or literary دخِى, is placed after the word of a phrase to which special attention is directed; thus : اِسْتَانُولْدَنْ دَخِى طُوبْ كَلْدِى) (ìstanbòldan dakhì, or ìstanbòdanda top galdì) *cannon came from Constantinople also;* اِسْتَانْبُولْدَنْ طُوبْ

دَخِى كَلْدِى (İstanboldan tóp dakhî galdî) *cannon, too, came from Constantinople.*

This enclitic is repeated after each member of a phrase linked together by its use; as, سَنْدَه بَدَرِم نِنْدَه (ben-da gederîm; san-da) *I, too, will go, as also thou;* بَنْدَه سَنْدَه اُولْدَه اُوچِمِز كَـدَرِز (ben-da, san-da, ó-da, uchumuz gíderîz) *I, thou, and he too, will all three go.*

It is often placed after a verb in the conditional, its sense being then, in English, rendered by *even ;* as, كَلْسَه دَه (galse-de) *even should he come ;* كَلْمِش اِسَه دَه (galmîsh îse-de) *even though he be come ;* كَلْسَیدِى دَه (galseydî-da) *had he even come ;* كَلَجَك اُولْسَه دَه (galejek ólsa-da) *even should he be about to come* (even should he think of coming, or resolve to come).

After other verbs than conditionals, it is enclitic with each that enters a phrase, and answers to our *both,* followed by *and* or *also;* as, كَلُورمَدَه كُورُرمَدَه (gelîrîm-da, gyururûm-da) *I will both come, and see also ;* (— , — , كَلُورمَدَه كُورُرمَدَه بَكْنُور اِسَمْ اَلُرِم الورمَدَه beyanîr-îse-m, alîrîm-da) *I will come, and I will see, and if I admire, will also buy.*

The conjunctions اِسْتَر, كِرَك, هَا , in the sense of *whether ... , or whether,* اَكَرْ (eyer) *if,* with كَرْچَه (ger-chî, *vulg.* gerche) or اَكَرْچَه (eyer-chî, *vulg.* egerche) *although,* put the verb or verbs of their phrase in the conditional ; as, هَا كَلْسَه هَا كَلْمَسَه (ha galse,

hâ galmasa) *whether he come, or* (whether he come) *not;* اَكْرَكَنَّه
(eyer galsa) *if he come;* اَكْرِجه اِيْسَدَه كَلْمِشْ (egerchi galmish isa-
da) *although he be even come* (even though he be come).

When the copulative و joins one verb or phrase to another,
it is pronounced ve, in couformity (to a certain degree) with
its original Arabic pronunciation; but when, in Persian construction, it unites two nouns, substautive or adjective, it takes
the vowel-sound of u or û, and joins on, in pronunciation, as
though in a syllable, with the consonant preceding it; as,
دولت و اقبال گَلْدِى و كَوْرْدِى (galdî ve gyurdu) *he came, and he saw;*
(devlet u iqbal) *fortune and prosperity;* قَوِى و تَنْدُرِسْت (qavi-yu
ten-durust) *strong and healthy.*

The Persian conjunction كِ (kî) *that,* always connects two
members of a phrase, and should never be supposed to be a
relative pronoun in Turkish (as it really is in Persian, as well
as a conjunction); as, مَعْلُومْ اُولَه كِه (ma'lum ola kî) *be it known
that ....* Sometimes the clause that follows shows the cause
or reason of that which precedes; the conjunction may then
be rendered by *for* or *because;* as, نِيَازْمَنْدْ اُولَهْلِمْ وَ نَالَه كُنَانْ كِه جِنْسْ
مَغْفَرَتِه سِيمْ اَشْكْ اُولْدِى نُقُودْ (niyâzmend ôlâlim, ve nale-kyunan, kî
jîns-i magferete sîm-i eshk ôldu nûqud) *let us be instant in sup-
plications, and assiduous in moans, for the silver of* (man's) *tears
has been made the coins payable for the wares of* (God's) *mercy.*
(The inversion نُقُودْ اُولْدِى for اُولْدِى نُقُودْ is poetical.)

After a verb signifying *to say* (which also may mean, *to say to one's self, to think*), or *to ask*, the conjunction كه introduces, what is, was, or will be said or thought; but the question must be in the mood, tense, number, and person, in the very words, used by the speaker or thinker; as, ديور ده يارين كلوره (dìyòr kì, yarìn gelìrìm) *he says, I will come to-morrow;* صوردی کـه بو نه د. (sòrdu kì, bu ne dìr) *he asked, What is this?* We see, then, that كه, so used, is the equivalent of our sign of quotation, the *inverted commas*. We cannot alter the phrase as is our custom, and say, *he says he will come*, or *he asked what that was*.

Occasionally, in a certain style, this كه is omitted; as, دیدی ای شهریار (dìdì: ey shehrìyar) *he exclaimed, "O monarch."*

But the method more generally used, especially in conversation, and which is the true Turkish mode, is to quote first what was said, asked, or thought, and then immediately to bring in the verb *to say, &c.*, in its proper tense, number, and person; as, كلورز دیورلر (gelìrìz dìyorler) *they say, We will come;* i. e., *they say they will come;* كورمدم دیدی (gyurmadìm dìdì) *he said, I did not see* (him, her, it, them, you, &c.); i. e., *he said he did not see.* In this case, if the verb used be any other than دیمك, the Turkish conjunction دیو (dìyu, *vulg.* deye), which really is the first or fifth gerund, modified by usage, of دیمك, *viz.*, دیوب or دده, is introduced before the verb used, and after the quotation; it is the equivalent of our *saying;* as, كیفکز ایوم دیو

سُؤَال اِتَّدَمْ (keyfínlz íyí-mí, díyú, suʾal etdím) *I asked* (of him or her), *saying, Is your health yood?* i. e., *I asked how he was;*

بلمَيورْزْ دِيو اِنْكَارْ اِدِيورلر (belmeyórlz, díyú, ínkyar ídíyórler) *they deny, saying, We know not;* i. e., *they deny, and say they know not;* كَلْمَزْسِكِزْ دِنُو خولِا اِتَّدَمْ (galmazsínlz, díyu, khulyá etdím) *I formed an idea, saying* (to myself), *You will not come;* i. e., *I imagined that you would not come;* نَه دِنُو كَلْدِيكِزْ (ne díyú, gál-dínlz) *saying what* (to thyself), *art thou come?* i. e., *what are you come for?*

The conjunction كَه sometimes, as in Persian, serves to connect an incidental qualifying phrase to an antecedent noun, as though it were a relative pronoun; but in such case it never undergoes declension or takes a preposition, the following phrase being complete in all its parts; as, حَمْدُ و سَاسْ اُولْ

خُدَاوَنْدِ بِي عِلَّتَه سَزَا دِرْكِه وُجُودِ اَنْهَارُ وقُعُورِ بِحَارْ يَكْقَطْرَءِ قُدْرَتِ نَامُتَنَاهِيلَرِي دِرْ

(hamd ú sípas ól khúdavend-í bí-ʾíllete seza dír, kí, vújud-í enhar u quʾur-í bíhar yek-qatre-í qudret-í na-mutenahíllerí dír) *glory and lauds are worthy of that uncaused Lord God, of whose infinite power the existence of rivers and the depths of oceans are but a single drop.*

The foregoing example shows that it is often difficult or impossible to distinguish whether the phrase that follows كِه is a qualificative, or the exposition of a reason. We might

take it in this latter sense, and translate: *for, the existence of
rivers, &c., are but one drop, &c.*

But, in ethical works and the like, generally composed by
members of the 'ûlemâ class (Doctors of Canon Law) on a
Persian or Arabic model, the clause that follows او is generally
qualificative, and the style is anti-Turkish. Thus : هَرْكَسْ كِه

دست همت ايده حبل متين عقله متشبث اوله (her kes ki dest-i himmet
ilâ habl-i metîn-i 'aqlâ mûteshebbis óla, ...) ; *every one who
shall take hold of the firm cable of reason with the hand of
endeavour, ...* ; بو حانورلر كه نظر عبرتله منظور در (bû janverler ki
nâzar-i 'îbret-lâ mânzur dûr, ...) *these animals which are
looked upon with a regard for instruction, ...*

The conjunctions تا كه (ta ki) *in order that*, شَايَد كه (shâyed
ki) *perhaps, lest*, مادامكه (mâ-dam-ki) *as long as, since*, مَبَادا كه
(me-badâ ki) *lest*, مَگَر او (meyer ki) *unless*, require their verbs
to be in the optative; as, تَا دَه تَحَمُّلِى قَالْمَیَه) tâhâmmûlu
qalmaya) *in order that no power of endurance be left in him* ;
شايد ده منهزم اولهلر (— — mûnhezim ólaler) *lest they be routed* ;
مادامكه حياتده اولهلر (hayâtdâ ólaler) *since they are alive* ;
مَگَر كه كوزَل اوله) ûylè olâ) *lest it be so* ; مبادا كه اويْلَه اوله
(gyuzel olâ) *unless he (she, it) be beautiful.*

SECTION XIII. *Syntax of the Interjection.*

Some interjections are accompanied by nouns and pronouns, some by nouns only, others have no accompaniment, and some precede verbs.

When accompanied by a noun, the noun is always in the nominative, excepting with the interjection نَازِق (yazîq) ; as, وَاخْ نَابَامْ (vwakh babam) *alas, my father !* آفَرِين أُوعُلُمْ (âferîn, *vulg.* aferîm oghlum) *well done, my boy !* سَدِى أَدَبْسِزْ (gîdî edeb-sîz) *O, impudent fellow !* آی قَردَاشِمْ (ey qardashîm) *well, brother !* آمَان چُوجُمْ (âman chojughum) *O, my child !* مَرْحَا ابِدمْ (merhaba efendîm) *God's blessing on you, sir !* They always precede the noun. The word نَازِق is used in this way also, but it further permits its substantive to be put in the dative ; as, نَازِق امَكَ (yazîq emeyîm), نَازِق امَكمَه (yazîq emeyîme) *alas my trouble ! alas for my trouble !*

When accompanied by a pronoun, except the interjection سَدِى (gîdî), the pronoun must be in the dative ; as, نَازِق سَكَا (yazîq bana) *poor me !* وَاخْ سَكَا (vwâkh sana) *alas for thee !* آفَرِين أَنْلَرَه (aferîm ânlarâ) *well done, they !* The exceptional سَدِى is constructed with the accusative of the second person singular, which it may precede or follow ; as, سَدِى سَنِى (gîdî sanî) or سَنِى سَدِى (sanî gîdî) *faugh, thou (good-for-nothing) !*

Interjections indicative of a desire for the future or regret for the past, are constructed with the conditional, aorist or past accordingly; as, آه كلسه (ah galsa) *O that he would come!* آه كلسه‌یدی (ah galseydī) *O that he had come!* One of these, آمان, is constructed also with the imperative, and expresses vehement desire with the affirmative, or dread with the negative; as, آمان كیتمسه (aman gitmasa) *O that he go not* (by his own desire)! آمان كیتمسین (āman gitmasin) *O that he go not* (if my wish prevail)!

With an imperative, هله (hele) expresses an invitation or a challenge; as, هله كل (hele gal) *come along!* هله كلسین (hele galsin) *just let him only come!*

Arabic phrases are often used as interjections, generally after proper names; as, مكّهٔ مكـّرمه،كرّمها اللّه تعالى (mekke-i mûkerreme, kerrema-ha 'llahù taala) *Mekka the Venerated, which may God, who be exalted, cause to be venerated!* سلطان غازی سلیم خان مدّ اللّه ظلال رأفته علی مفارق الأنام ما تكرّر الشهور و تجدّد الأعوام حضرتلری *His Majesty, the champion of the faith, Sultan Selim Khan, the shadows of whose clemency may God spread over the crowns of the heads of mankind, so long as the months repeat themselves and the years renew themselves!*

FINIS.

ADDENDUM.

In p. 45, after line 5, as a further remark on the uses of letter و, the following rule is not without its use; viz.,—

In a few words of Persian origin only, the letter و, following a letter خ, and itself followed by a long vowel-letter ا, is suppressed and lost in the pronunciation. Thus خوان kh'ān, خواه. kh'ah, خواهش kh'ahsh. The word خواجه kh'aja, of this class, and its derivatives, خواجهلق , حواحکان , &c., have been corrupted in Turkish into khoja, khojagyan, khojalíq, &c. In Persian proper, a very few words beginning with خو, without a following ا, elide the و in like manner in pronouncing; but this is never observed in Turkish, unless it may be in the rhyme-words of ancient poetry. Thus the word خوش (usually read khush in Persian, khósh in Turkish) is made to rhyme with وش vesh, for instance; and in consequence must then be read kh'ash. خود (usually khud, Turkish khód) is made to rhyme with بد bed; something after the manner of our poets, who make *wind* rhyme with *find*, *mind*, &c. This is what is styled واو معدوله (vwāwî ma'dule), *deflected* و, in Persian.

INDEX.

London : Gilbert & Rivington, Limited, St. John's Sq., Clerkenwell Road.

Made in the USA
Las Vegas, NV
09 October 2022

56884062R00122